The Hypocrisy

Of

America

Table of Contents

Dedications

This book is dedicated to all my friends, and family. I appreciate you all.

For all those who died or have lost a loved one to cancer or any other horrible disease.

For all those who are fighting for justice.

For all those fighting for freedom.

For all those who feel powerless.

For those who are helping others.

For those who can't help themselves.

I have a t-shirt company called Tortured Tees. The motto is, "Tortured Tees, for the tortured soul in all of us." I feel we all have our own inner demons we battle. Even when we look like we have everything together, and we are happy, some of us have a daily battle we fight with ourselves. This book is for you too.

www.facebook.com/torturedtees

AMERICA: THE WAR MACHINE
Forward by Kenneth Cosentino

James and I have been friends for a long time now; I met him right after he got out of federal prison. We met at his brother's boxing gym located above a tattoo parlor. He was quiet, reserved, a hell of a fighter, and observant of everything that was going on in the room. Today we own a company together, White Lion Studios, LLC, and we both founded the original company Little Sicily Productions in 2009. Last year, I ran a political campaign in my hometown for the only grassroots candidate on the slate; Bill Kennedy, our company president and brother. Bill won top vote and is now a seated Niagara Falls city councilman. Together we unseated Governor Andrew Cuomo's publicly endorsed eight-year incumbent. What is a state governor doing interfering with local city elections and how many cities in New York State, come election time, can say that Cuomo sends money, people and resources to support a candidate? Truth be told the whole system is corrupt and I saw it first hand in my dealings with politicians and their handlers on many levels. Running a political campaign became more of a revolution as we played a big game of chess with the professionals who put politicians in office for a living. With Bill as our candidate, we won that chess game. James taught me how to play chess. He also introduced me to the musical stylings of Tom Waits, so right there you are either going to love this book or hate it.

While reading the book, I picture James telling me this story from the boxing gym, or inside a prison cell, or in a courtroom. His writing style flows from a passionate and well-informed rant; to personal journey full of lessons; to board room brawler - Wolf of Wall Street motherfucker - with a narrative reminiscent of Goodfellas. Let me tell you - this guy is dangerous. He's dangerous in a sense that he knows what the fuck he's talking about and he's not going to limit his words, or play to the egos of public figures. I have spent time in a boxing ring with James and we've gone to war together on several of our film productions. Few people are as knowledgeable as he is about what's going on in our country and society. He's got his finger on the pulse of corruption and with this book it looks like he's going to strangle it.

The first thing I can think to tell you is: Follow the money trail. Corporations are running this country. Hell, the United States of America is a corporation located around Washington D.C. In 1791, the District of Columbia was ceded to the federal government for the purpose of becoming the nation's capital, to be governed by Congress. What's the opposite of Progress? Congress. According to the 10th Amendment of the Constitution, all powers not granted to the federal government are reserved for the states and the people. D.C. residents have only been able to vote for President since 1964. Whereas states appoint their own judges, the President appoints judges for District Court.

The President acts as CEO of the American Corporation, but the biggest problem is the Federal Reserve.

We are borrowing money from private bankers who trade us bonds with interest. If we borrow $100 and they print all of our money, they have to print an additional debt to pay the interest. So our country is perpetually in debt, it's not broken; it's how the system was designed. It is a system of debt and after FDR's New Deal, we became collateral. The reason we have social security and a national census is so the government knows how much the country is worth in assets because we are weighed against the World Stock Exchange. We the taxpayers support this ridiculous shit and the result is the decimation of the class system from upper, middle and lower to upper, working class and poor. These are the final days of capitalism and 1% of the most elite billionaires in the world are collecting all debts.

I say this with utmost assurance given the gravity of the situation; Donald Trump is President of the United States of America. Capitalism as we know it will not survive climate change. Much of our economy is supported by energy companies in the coal and oil businesses, and these same moguls are the ones pulling the strings globally. Lobbyists and unions are both corrupted and both have more political sway than every man, woman and child on this soil. The system is not broken, it is designed to be a Democratic front for capitalism. Capitalism has poisoned our Democracy. Money is not the root of all evil; the love of money is. These same corporations are mega-conglomerates and they also own most major media outlets, Hollywood, and they're partnered with banks. I worked as a legal assistant at a law firm that handles mortgages, bankruptcies and foreclosures. In that time, I saw the bowels of the ship we call America. I saw how banks open lending services

6

with appealing titles like Financial Freedom and The Money Source. My job was to proofread documents and I was absolutely floored when I read the authentication stamps from certain banks which stated "BIG BANK UNDER THE FICTITIOUS NAME OF AMERICAN WHOLESALE LENDER." How does one sell mortgages wholesale?

Lawyers and office managers spoke openly about the absolute corruption, but most showed no remorse for the borrowers because "They shouldn't have signed the contract." I saw the inner workings of the systems compiling all of the data for every single borrower from every bank that the firm worked with. Basically it was a collection agency and the lowest rung of work for an attorney. Banks own the property and the borrower takes out a bank loan to purchase the property from the bank. Let's say a house is sold for $100,000; you take out a mortgage to pay for the $100,000 but the full loan is not given to you - the house is. So you don't really see a penny of that loan but you pay it with interest in order to live in the house. Banks don't have money to loan out, they use our money. These days it's all digital so who knows if that money is actually sitting in the bank or if there is a CEO somewhere on their yacht surrounded by high priced hookers. Half of my time at the law firm was spent in the vault and I imagined myself setting fire to everyone's mortgages. I probably would have done it too, had I not been told that the original document was no longer necessary for the mortgage to remain valid (they have something called a "lost note affidavit" which ruined my diabolical scheme).

The banks may own the property, but the government

claims ownership over the land. Land ownership is the biggest scam and the most common form of colonization right after raping and pillaging. Soon comes enslavement; whether it be slaves in shackles or wage slaves, the difference is the former know they are shackled. Along with enslavement comes conformity (the United States educational institution is just as corrupt as the healthcare system) preying off of the sick is, in itself, a mental illness. So who is it that is perpetrating this mental illness? Psychopaths. The world is run by psychopaths who lack empathy; and so, when made aware that their new pipeline will run through protected land and poison the only water source for the Natives, the CEO for Big Oil doesn't flinch. Truthfully, it's all about Manifest Destiny. It's still going on today, right in front of our eyes. Race wars, the war on drugs, terrorism; all of it is meant to fuel America's number 1 export: War. If I had written this book, I would have called it "America: The War Machine" because that's what it all boils down to. Our main business is conquering other countries, assassinating their leaders and installing Democratic Capitalism. The long arm of Johnny Law extends overseas in our military industrial complex. We produce bullets, missiles, planes, tanks, bombs, etc. and then we create the need for more! Supply and demand, business is booming.

So then, what can we do about all of this? Well first and foremost we must be informed of our rights and well informed of what the hell is going on. The government does not give us our rights, we are born with rights. The government is "supposed" to protect those rights. It says so right in the Constitution. That's what the whole Democracy "thing" is "supposed" to be about. Historically, different dynasties have held power within this system. The Bushes, Clintons, Rothschilds, etc. are all dynasties. The Clinton Dynasty took a devastating blow from Donald Trump who is representing his rich friends that are sucking what little life is left from our economy.

This book does an excellent job of bringing the uninformed, average individual up to date with the reality that we are currently experiencing. Consider this: If you were in charge, would you still be following the 40 hour work week? Why would we create a system, based on 24 hours a day, where we are meant to sleep 8 hours, work 8 hours and have 8 hours of recreation? Does it actually work this way? Hell no, it does not! People typically get less than 8 hours of sleep, work more than 8 hours a day and spend the rest of their time drunk, on drugs or zoned out in front of the television, trying to ignore the piling debt from being taxed to death. This is how they keep you sedated so that you don't revolt. Who has time to start a revolution when we all have nine-to-fives and bills to pay? Why is it illegal to collect rain water? What the fuck is that about?! It falls from the sky and it collects naturally, but if we put out a barrel to catch it and store it, somebody's gotta get paid??

The 13th Amendment states: Neither slavery nor involuntary servitude, <u>except as a punishment for crime</u> whereof the party shall have been duly convicted, shall exist within the United States or any place subject to their jurisdiction. Slavery still exists today, it's just made legal by unjust conviction. James does an excellent job of explaining this fact from the point of view of someone who was "inside."

December 4th, 2016, former President Obama halted the Dakota Access Pipeline (DAPL) after public outcry in support of the Standing Rock Water Protectors safety. Of course, it was just a show of humanity on his part. It didn't stick. January 24th, 2017, President Trump reversed the halt, expediting the environmental review which he described as an "incredibly cumbersome, long, horrible permitting process." On February 7th, Trump authorized the Army Corps of Engineers to proceed. February 23rd, law enforcement assisted by the National Guard evicted anyone who was left at Standing Rock. DAPL was constructed, declaring victories for the untouchable elite billionaires who invested in Energy Transfer Partners and the pipeline (including Trump himself); vicious mercenaries such as TigerSwan who declared war on Sioux soil against American citizens gathering in protest and prayer; and the outright racist Morton County justice (Just Us) department who saw an opportunity to beat up some Indians. In all of that, when these events were happening in real time, on January 21st and 22nd an estimated 500,000–1,000,000 people protested in Washington, D.C. at the Women's Rights March. It was an anti-Trump extravaganza where women dressed in gigantic pink foam vagina costumes and shouted their disapproval that *he is not their president*. Had these people instead rerouted to Standing Rock where those at the front needed them, history would be different. Hillary fans were in it for the photo opportunity, but there are those of us who actually want to see change in the status quo.

10

So, I will leave you with this: Vote with your dollar. If you are endorsing corporations that are destroying our planet and making us sick, find a small privately owned company to buy from instead. Keep money circulating locally by shopping with local businesses. Take this book, not as entertainment, but as a guide to bettering your life. Remove the rose-colored glasses from your face and join the revolution, we need all the help that we can get. What Mr. Ventry has done here by compiling data and citing all of his sources is a great service to the betterment of mankind, and I'm proud to call him my brother.

~ *Ken Cosentino*
11/27/2018

Introduction

I started thinking about writing this book during the first Bush administration. As what often happens with me, I get inspired or angry, and then the feeling goes away or other projects get in the way, and I never ended up following through. As each issue sort of came and went, I would always think, "well, you blew it, your book idea won't be relevant now." Sadly, though month after month, year after year the premise of this book keeps being relevant.

The premise of this book is to dispel a myth we are taught as children. It's an idea that is implanted in us and to a large extent we are brainwashed with this idea. At some point in our lives, many of us come to realize that what we were taught was the ultimate truth was nothing more than the ultimate lie. What is this myth? It's the simple belief that everything America does is just. If we are doing something as a nation, it must be "just" because it's for the betterment of the world. We're America, home of the brave, land of the free. We're America, the freest country in the world. We're America, we set the standard for human rights. We're America, the red, white, and blue my friend. We wouldn't be doing something if it weren't right; Right? Some people, somehow, never open their eyes to the realization this is only a myth. I'm referring to the Bill O'Reilly's, the Rush Limbaugh's; every right wing, conservative Republican; every blue loving, no-matter-what voting Democrat; every gun-toting hillbilly and, well, actually, almost everyone.

I think very few people have the ability to see the truth. They blindly go on believing in the righteousness of America. They believe in our government's right to incarcerate endless amounts of Americans without having to prove their crimes. Well, Rush Limbaugh may have changed his mind about this after his little prescription drug charges, but probably only when it concerns himself. They believe in our right to detain individuals in the name of national security while believing those detained do not even have the right to know why or how long they are being detained for. They believe in our right to invade foreign countries or overthrow governments who won't allow our corporations to steal their natural resources, but not in our right as citizens to question those reasons or the right. They believe in our governments right to strip the constitution of all it's meaning while boasting we are the freest country in the world.

Even U.S. citizens don't seem to be in favor of freedoms when it's someone else who does not share the same belief as them. From liberals who protest speakers they disagree with to the typical slightly racist individuals who are so angry at those kneeling during our national anthem. When I first started thinking about writing this book I was planning on starting with our governments policy of genocide towards Native Americans, and working my way up to slavery, and the black mark on our constitution. I would continue my writing with in depth looks at all our immoral acts as a country. That would have been a book written similar to an author like a Stephen Ambrose, but obviously much more critical of the U.S. than Mr. Ambrose ever wrote. I love political commentary, and satire. Being big fans of both Michael Moore, and Al Franken I decided to write a book more in their style. I thought it would have broader appeal, allow me to focus on subjects that are more important to me, and lastly give me an opportunity to call people like Rush Limbaugh, Sean Hannity, Tucker Carlson and of course Donald Trump all assholes. In doing so, not only would I have fun, but possibly Michael and Al would become fans of mine.

I thought living through the Bush years were bad. I even broke up with a girl I was going out with because she thought he was a great President. No matter how hard I tried I couldn't get it through her head that Iraq had nothing to do with the 9/11 attacks. With the creation of the Patriot Act we lost some freedoms under President Bush. Free speech was under attack big time. On April 23rd 2004 Secret Service agents interrogated a 15 year old high school student in Prosser, Washington for making anti-warsketches for his art class. This is the sort of thing you think about happening in communist China, not the United States of America. Thomas Jefferson once said "A society that will trade a little liberty for a little order will deserve neither and lose both." In general President Trump makes me long for President Bush (although Bush/Cheney did far more real world damage), and free speech is something President Trump is only in favor of if he likes who is speaking, and what they are saying. The act of kneeling would be considered free speech, and we know how Trump feels about that. I would never burn the flag, but I don't think it should be against the law either. Trump once tweeted "Nobody should be allowed to burn the American flag – if they do, there must be

consequences – perhaps loss of citizenship or a year in jail!"
Worse than all of that President Trump has called journalists
an "enemy of the American People." Wow, no President
should ever feel comfortable with saying such nonsense.
Although, there never has been another President more
comfortable with uttering more nonsense than President
Trump.

I'm not writing this book for scholars who already
know much of this information. I'm writing it for the slightly
above average, curious, American. I wrote "slightly above
average" American because I'm afraid the "average"
American doesn't have much desire to read these days. I
love my country. That being, said I don't love it blindly, and
I certainly have zero trust for our government. This is not
the country our four fathers envisioned. We have lost
freedoms, and becoming more and more of a totalitarian
state every day. Now we have a fascist leader with a cult-
like following who are clearly unable to think for themselves
at all. We are in more danger than ever of moving further,
and further away from our American myth.
You may not agree with this because you get to
watch your television, drink your beer, and for the most part
no one bothers you. I have a house in Niagara Falls that I
had on Airbnb for a short period of time, and I met people
from countries such as Italy, Canada, Spain, and France to
name a few, and they all told me this is the most policed
nation they have ever visited. From the time you wake up to
the time you go to bed, to the time you wake up again there
is no aspect of your life the government does not touch. You
may not be aware, and of course much of what they regulate

is good, but there is no doubt the government is ever present in our lives. Besides working for corporations, our government runs, and supports the two most immoral jobs programs there is in the Military Industrial Complex, and the Prison Industrial Complex. We have approximately 25% of the world's prison population while only representing just under 5% of the world's population. As Americans, we are either the worst lot of people on the face of the planet or our government is way too intrusive. It's one or the other, so which is it?

The ideals of this country are beautiful. With every civil liberty lost this country loses some of its beauty. With every individual locked up for long periods of time for minor crimes this country losessome of its humanity. With every act of tyranny throughout the world our government loses some of its credibility. As a society if we don't step up, and make our government accountable, then the dream of America will be just that, a dream, and the myth of America will forever be our reality.

Chapter 1-

Trump, Hillary, and Bernie

I've been a Bernie fan for many years so when I first heard he was running for President I was very excited. I told anyone, and everyone who would listen everything I knew about Bernie. In the early stages that's all I ever heard was that he had no chance of beating Hillary. I suppose early on I had my doubts as well, but I also had a belief that he had to win. This was nothing short of a once and a lifetime opportunity. I'm grateful that we live in an era where information is everywhere, and can be seen in real time. I would see videos of Bernie rallies with thousands of energized people. You wouldn't have known that if you watched the news because they were dead set on it being Hillary's turn to run for, and win the Presidency. I'm positive if this had been 10 or 15 years ago we would have never been aware of the grass roots movement that was taking place because the national media mostly ignored Bernie, and we would have not known any better. Eventually, Bernie would have had to get out of the race because people like myself would have given up. We would have thought we were the only ones who knew about Bernie, unaware there were thousands who were dying for real change.

The DNC, and the media did everything they could to help Hillary. Donna Brazile, who was the interim chair of the Democratic National Committee, leaked debate questions and topics to Hillary. These leaked debate questions should have been a huge story for the rest of the primary race, but it was almost dead immediately. Brazile thought she was doing her duty as the DNC chair, and she would do it again if that's what was necessary. During a radio interview with Sirius XM host Joe Madison, Brazile stated "if I had to do it all over again, I would know a hell of a lot more about cybersecurity." CNN had no choice but to fire Brazile, but her punishment for betraying the voters, and democracy itself can never be enough. I don't understand why this was brushed aside like it wasn't that big of a deal. Brazile admitted in an interview with the Washington Post that although she should be neutral she was not, and indeed she was "ready for Hillary." What bothered me even more about this scandal was Hillary Clinton was completely let off the hook for this. They remained silent in the days after the scandal hit the news, and the media helped by not really being or remaining outraged. I don't think Bernie did himself any favors by being the class act he is. Bernie failed to take advantage of this issue among other issues as he refused to truly go after Hillary. I think even Bernie was worried that if he lost and damaged Hillary too much it would help Trump win. I think that was the prevailing thought for many nationally known individuals who "supported" Bernie.

Bill Maher is someone I admire, and respect so much, and who could have easily helped Bernie much more than he did. I think Mr. Maher is the best example I can find in how he felt, and behaved while semi supporting Bernie. Mr. Maher refused to ever criticize Hillary for fear he would damage her, and thus help Trump. If he would have went all in for Bernie, I believe Mr. Maher would have helped keep the media a little more honest. Mr. Maher should have been all in for Bernie, and he wasn't. Even now every time someone speaks and disagrees with something that happened with Bernie, Mr. Maher cuts the person speaking right off. Being a huge Bill Maher fan, I watch Bill on HBO week in, and week out. Often, if not always, when someone speaks poorly, and truthfully about Hillary or anyone in the Democratic Party, Mr. Maher talks over them, and refuses to let them speak. I see that often on his show with him or if he has someone on his show like Barney Frank. Mr. Frank will speak over more liberal voices, and turn into a bully right before our very eyes. Mr. Frank did this on Maher's August 3rd show regarding Whistleblowers. Even Maher jokingly stated "You're badgering the witness Barney." Frank gives paid speeches to Wall Street now, and claimed it's because "He's interesting" and of course defended Hillary for her paid speeches. Where does Mr. Barney Frank work now? Barney was elected on the board of directors for Signature Bank. Frank is another hypocrite that takes advantage of the influence he will have because of his former job. In an interview with the "Observer" Frank states "The notion that banks are too influential--I think this is a mistake on part of some of my friends on the left, and maybe in general. The big banks do not have the political influence that people think they do." Okay Barney, how do you even say that bullshit without laughing your ass off? I recently watched a video where another person I truly admire, Cornell West, was criticizing Obama, and Al Sharpton was yelling over him so he could drown out the truth. I don't understand why you can't tell the truth about what someone is doing just because they are perceived to be on the same team as you.

Once the DNC, and media got the Hillary victory they wanted, they thought all of us Bernie supporters should just jump on board the Hillary train. I can't tell you how angry this made almost all of us Bernie supporters. I will never forget the time Sarah Silverman said to the Bernie or Bust people "You're being ridiculous" then she went on the Bill Maher show, and Mr. Maher tells Sara Silverman he thought it was wonderful. It blows my mind how Bill, and Sarah just do not get it. Let me see if I can explain this to you Bill; We live in a semi free country, and we all get to make many choices. I was a high school teacher for a little while, and when I would give a test some kids would complain, and say they didn't want to take it. I would tell them, "You don't have to take the test, as a matter of fact you don't even have to stay here in class if you chose not to." I would tell the students "You are free to get up right now and leave. Of course the act of leaving may come with a consequence." So Hillary, and the DNC stole the primary election from Bernie, then you want us to pretend it didn't happen. Not only do you want us to pretend it didn't happen, but you want us to reward them for their behavior! No way, not a chance in hell were we going to do that! If we did they would do the same thing that they have always done. Now for us, we understood that there would also be a consequence for us refusing to vote for Hillary, but we were willing to accept that. No way were we voting for Hillary, consequences be damned. We ended up with the horrible, horrible
20

consequence of Donald Trump being elected our President. Even though we had to suffer the consequence, it was not our fault, it was yours! It was the DNC's! It was Hillary's!

Killer Mike was recently on Bill Maher, and he explained nicely why he couldn't switch over to Hillary. Killer Mike stated "I saw a guy get robbed, and for all that was moral, and good about me I couldn't un-see that." Then, of course what did Bill do, he got mad, and really didn't let Killer Mike finish everything he wanted to say. Mike talked about how active Bernie has been, and how Bernie has "been in the streets" and how Hillary hasn't "been in the streets" and Bill cut him off. Fran Lebowitz was another recent Maher guest who spoke disrespectfully about Bernie calling him a narcissist. What!? Bernie is about "we" not "I" and that is why we were all Bernie or Bust. So guess what Fran, you're the narcissist, so fuck you, fuck Hillary, and most of all, fuck the DNC.

I participated in politics for the first time because of Bernie. I have always loved politics, I love debating, and having discussions, but I never actually participated. This was the first time I donated, and donated multiple times. This is the first time I went to political rallies, and also met with other Bernie supporters. Bernie inspired myself and millions of others.

Let's take a look at Hillary's record: In 2002 Hillary voted for the Iraq war. You all already know where Bernie stood on this issue. Like always, Bernie is on the right side of history before most others in our government are. Bernie leads, Hillary follows, and usually what Hillary follows is the money. Hillary spoke multiple times to Goldman Sachs, Morgan Stanley, Deutsche Bank, Kohlberg Kravis Roberts, and UBS Wealth Management for a whopping $225,000 each speech. Mrs. Clinton didn't just sell out to Wall Street, she also betrays us by taking huge sums of money for her speeches to the Pharmaceutical industry. The National Association of Chain and Drug Stores, and the Healthcare Information and Management Systems Society both paid the hefty $225,000 dollar fee as well. I think we all understand that unless it's a roast, no one pays someone to say things they do not want to hear. What did she say? Who knows, and she will never release the speeches so until someone steals them we won't ever know what Hillary told her Wall Street friends. Hillary was on the side of President Bush on homeland security as well, and voted for the Patriot Act. Want to guess who didn't? I bet you guessed it, yep, Bernie. In case you thought she got caught up after 9/11 like she did with voting for the Iraq war, and once time passed Hillary was able to access the situation and rethink her position; you'd be wrong. When votes to renew the legislation in 2005 and 2006 came up, Hillary again voted in favor, while Bernie voted against. None of this is anything new, but it's the stuff Hillary supporters don't want to hear about or speak about. I'm glad Killer Mike, and Cornell West are two African Americans who didn't support Hillary because most African American communities have been fooled by the Democrats, and by the Clintons as well. Under Bill Clinton, funding for public housing decreased by $17 billion. Funding for corrections (which would cause African American families to be torn apart again) increased by 19 billion. For some reason our government seems to always find different ways to separate African Americans from the rest of us. I will cover this much more in my chapter about prisons, and also race. I love Bill Maher. I even went to see him this past winter (early 2018) when Bill performed at Shea's in Buffalo, NY. I think for the most part Trump has reinvigorated Bill to being the old Bill again except for those times where he shows me he still just doesn't get it when it comes to the Bernie supporters, and how we would never support Hillary, no matter what the consequence. Lastly, I see Hillary pop back up occasionally, and it's the last thing this country needs. I think she would love to run for President again, and is putting herself out there to see what people think. Soooooo, please, go crawl under a rock, and go away for about 7 or 8 years.

So now we are dealing with the consequence, which is the nightmare Presidency of Donald Trump. We are reminded daily because with each new day, comes a new scandal, a new embarrassing tweet, or some other controversy involving Trump or one of his moronic supporters. It's almost impossible to keep up with the news and scandals coming out of the Trump White House. I'm trying to write this book, and the news is moving at lighting speed every day. I have to keep telling myself "I'm not a newspaper. I can't keep addressing every scandal that comes out of the White House or I will never finish." The speed at which the news is moving makes me believe, or hope President Trump will be impeached by the time this book gets published. However, life goes on, and so I will plot forward, and hope for the best just as I did when Mr. Trump was running for President. During the race for the President

I was honestly hopeful that if Trump won he wouldn't actually do anything he was saying, and that the mentally challenged Trump supporters would be very disappointed. I should have known better because Trump made his entrance into the current political landscape by continually claiming or wondering aloud if Obama had really been born in the United States. Perhaps it was with this attack on then President Obama where Mr. Trump first discovered his base. However, to spite this ridiculous claim there were still many reasons for me to hold on to my hope. On Meet the Press in 1999 while speaking to Tim Russert, Mr. Trump stated it wouldn't bother him at all if homosexuals served openly in the military. Mr. Trump went on, and spoke about how he "is strongly for choice" concerning the subject of abortion. When it comes to the abortion issue I think Trump feels like many liberal minded people; we don't like abortions, but we are pro-choice. Now Trump is stacking the Supreme Court with Justices who may attempt to overturn Roe v. Wade. We all know what is happening with Brett Kavanaugh, who is currently home drinking beers. Hopefully President Trump will have to nominate another asshole for the Supreme Court, but a slightly less rapey, drunk asshole. What people who want to overturn Roe v. Wade fail to realize is making abortions illegal won't stop abortions from taking place. Unfortunately, abortions will move from the safety of a medical facility, performed by a doctor, to someone's house performed by Donald Trump with a hanger. Who knows, these backwards assholes may try to overturn the Thirteenth Amendment. I think the only amendment that is truly safe is the infamous Second Amendment.

24

Trump himself often had high opinions of the Democrats. In a 2004 interview with CNN's Wolf Blitzer, Mr. Trump stated "It just seems the economy does better under Democrats than the Republicans." In another interview with the same Wolf Blitzer this time in 2007, Trump actually praised Hillary Clinton. Mr. Trump felt Hillary would do a great job, be a tough negotiator, and could successfully work out a deal with Iran. Trump went on to state "Hillary's always surrounded herself with very good people. I think Hillary would do a good job." When it came to guns Mr. Trump's views for the most part were that of the mainstream. In Trump's book, "The America We Deserve", Trump writes "I generally oppose gun control, but I support the ban on assault weapons, and I also support a slightly longer waiting period to purchase a gun." Those are views most Americans can live with, and agree with too. Health care is another issue Donald covered, and believe it or not Mr. Trump was also on the liberal side in "The America We Deserve". Covering the health care issue, Mr. Trump writes "We should not hear so many stories of families ruined by health care expenses. We must not allow citizens with medical problems to go untreated because of financial problems or red tape." Trump goes on to write "The Canadian plan also helps Canadians live longer, and healthier than America. We need, as a nation, to reexamine the single-payer plan, as many individual states are doing." So what happened to this level-headed Donald Trump? I think as the Republican primaries got rolling he found what worked, and he went with it. At first I don't think Trump believed anything he was saying. I think if he lost he would have come clean, and said he only said those things because he knew he was appealing to all those hillbilly, crazy Republicans. Trump would have confessed he really believes they are a bunch of fools. I have a brother who is unfortunately a huge Trump fan, and I used to tell him all the time, "Trump doesn't believe anything he's saying. Trump is just saying those things because he knows it gets people like you all fired up, and if he loses he's going to admit he didn't believe anything he said." The problem with Donald Trump is he's been playing the role now for so long he has now become the character he was only playing at the start. I think now Trump actually believes in the bullshit he spews because he played the part so well, for so long, he's morphed into that over the top, crazy Donald Trump. I've heard of this type of thing happening to method actors. They get so intensely into a role that they have a hard time de-characterizing. Trump has become the character he was playing, and unfortunately for most of us the character he is playing is a crazy, monster. That's not to say, Trump was some amazing, kind person prior to the election, but I honestly do not believe he was ever as horrible as he is now.

One aspect of his Presidency that is a part of his true character because he's a spoiled rich kid is his undoing of everything fantastic President Obama achieved. It's become his most important personal mission. We all know it started at the 2011 White House correspondent's dinner where President Obama roasted Mr. Trump for about five straight minutes. Obama being a fantastic orator was a natural, and because this was after Trump's birther bullshit, Obama truly enjoyed crushing Trump. Mr. Trump would never admit this but, believe me the "N" word was being thrown around all night at the Trump residence that evening. The comical speech was so good some of it needs to be revisited here. "No one is happier, no one is prouder to put this birth certificate matter to rest than the Donald. That's because he can finally get back to focusing on the issues that matter, like: Did we fake the moon landing? What really happened in Roswell? And where are Biggie and Tupac?" The lines received huge laughs, and Donald was seething on the inside. Trust me, "N" word all night! President Trump is a 70 something year old child. President Trump is a complete embarrassment. I don't blame many people who wanted Trump to win the election. Hillary was a horrible candidate. Bernie should have been the Democratic nominee. I didn't want someone who has never met a war she didn't love to win. Hillary inspired those who hate her much more than those who liked her. Many reluctantly supported her, but it stemmed from the dislike of Trump rather than wanting Hillary as their President. The issue I have with someone who was a Trump supporter is that if you supported him prior to the election, and now after seeing his behavior, after reading his tweets, after witnessing his policies, and then you still support him; To me, that says something about you as a person. I still have my Bernie for President bumper sticker on my back windshield. Sometimes someone will ask me; why is it that I still have the Bernie sticker on my car? I explain it's because the Bernie bumper sticker says something about who I am as a person. It's not about Bernie. It's about inclusion, tolerance, and love. It says, I'm not a racist. It says, I care about others. Most importantly, it says, I'm not a dick. (Even though, truth be told, sometimes I am ☺). A Trump bumper sticker says the complete opposite, and those who drive with a Trump bumper sticker on are either too stupid to know that's what it means, or they are too much of an asshole to even care.

Trump's cult members also do not care about facts. He can tweet something or be recorded on film making a statement, then the next day Mr. Trump can say it never happened, its fake news, and his supporters believe him. I've never seen anything like it. Mr. Trump correctly understood the stupidity of his supporters when at a rally in Sioux Center, Iowa, Trump stated "I could stand in the middle of Fifth Avenue and shoot somebody, okay, and I wouldn't lose any voters, okay? It's like, incredible". Trump was basically calling his stupid followers "stupid" right to their face, but they were actually too stupid to realize it.

Let's take a look at a few of Trump's policies starting with the tax cuts. The Trump tax cuts changed the corporate tax rate from 35% to 21%. The top rate of those earning $500,000 and up drops from 39.6% to 37%. The corporate tax cuts have no end date, while the individual tax cuts are set to expire in 2026. First off that corporate rate of 35% is bullshit. Apple reports paying a tax rate of 25.8%, Microsoft 16.5%, Alphabet, which is the parent company of Google paid 19%. Twenty six Fortune 500 firms paid no federal income taxes at all from 2008 to 2012 including General Electric. General Electric seems to always find a way to continue to not only pay no taxes, but to receive a tax benefit. Last year General Electric earned a nice 10 billion dollars while receiving 400 million dollar tax benefit, thus achieving a tax rate of -4.5%!!! That should infuriate Trumpers, but instead they are mad at the person working 30 hours a week at the Walmart collecting food stamps. There is a common misconception that corporations flip the bill for most of the federal taxes collected. That's just simply not true. Individuals like you, and I contribute the largest portion of tax revenue. Income taxes contribute just below $1.7 trillion dollars, or about 50% while another one-third comes from your payroll taxes. Prior to the Trump tax cuts, corporations only paid 9% of the federal income taxes collected, and that will now drop to 7%. Those poor corporations, they had it rough. As a matter of fact those corporations have it so rough they actually hide over two trillion dollars in cash overseas. It blows my mind how greedy people who run corporations are.

Gas, and Oil companies get huge tax breaks for basically looking for, and drilling for the product they sell. That would be like incentivizing McDonald's for searching for cows for their hamburgers. U.S. taxpayers subsidize the oil, and gas industry's business from the start to the finish. In 2016 Exxon Mobile received a $406 million income tax benefit! It's disgusting, and we can actually go back to Bill Clinton's Presidency to when he signed the Deep Water Royalty Relief Act. This act waived the 12% royalty fee Big Oil would have owed once they found oil off our Gulf Coast.

Again though Trump's cult members are mad at a single mother getting some help, not the billions going to corporate welfare.

In the end the Trump tax cuts will help himself, and other wealthy individuals now, and into the future much more than it will ever help the middle class. An average middle class family will only save about $1,000.00 on their taxes, and as mentioned earlier, the tax cut for the middle class expires in 2026. A family in the top 1% would save approximately $215,000 while a family who are in the top 0.1% would save over 1 million dollars. I know you're thinking, "well they pay more so they are going to save more, so who cares?" Well, in my opinion they don't need to have any tax savings. When someone earns enormous sums of money they can pay higher taxes. It's for the betterment of our entire country, and individuals, and corporations have to stop being so selfish and greedy.

Trump signed 96 Laws in his first year. Can you imagine if he knew Obama signed 124 Laws in his first year? Trump would have signed anything to get to 125. Trump would have signed a law stating Toney's could not eat tacos on Tuesdays. Poor Toney's. President Trump being the consistent liar he is stated in a speech to first responders in West Palm Beach, Florida "We have more legislation passed, including the record- was Harry Truman. That's a long time ago. And we broke that record. So we have a lot done." Well, unless you're including Obama, Bush, Clinton, H.W.

Bush, Reagan, Carter, Nixon, Kennedy and Eisenhower. One thing President Trump truly has excelled at is telling lies. The Washington Post had President Trump making 3,001 untrue statements at the time I first wrote this. Now in the Washington Post's August 1st, 2018 article, the Post has President Trump making 4,229 false or misleading claims in 558 days in office. That is an average of almost 8 lies or misleading statements each and every day! I've been debating on putting many of President Trump's lies in here, but I suppose Trump's lies would take about 20 or 30 pages alone. In honor of David Letterman I think I will do a top 10 though. I was a big Letterman fan back when he was at the top of his game.

Number 10. "The overall audience was, I think, the biggest ever to watch an inauguration address, which was a great thing." (Sorry, estimates are put at about 600,000 ouch, you lost to Obama again who had about 1.8 million). **Number 9.** "I never said Russia did not meddle in the election, I said 'it may be Russia, or China (Jina, Jina, ☺) or another country or group, or it may be a 400 pound genius sitting in bed, and playing with his computer." (Trump called it "Fake News" and in an interview with Time Magazine, President Trump stated "I don't believe they interfered"). **Number 8.** "The 2018 defense authorization bill includes raises for the military for the first time in 10 years." (I only wish this were true). **Number 7.** "In many places, like California the same person votes many times. You probably heard about that. They always like to say 'oh that's a conspiracy theory.' Not a conspiracy theory, folks. Millions, and millions of people." (It was two people Donald; Beavis and Butthead, you dumbass). **Number 6.** "Terrible! Just found out that Obama had my 'wires tapped' in Trump Tower just before the victory. Nothing found. This is McCarthyism!" (All the racist Obama haters still probably believe that bs). **Number 5.** "Obamacare covers very few people." (Only if you consider approximately 10 million people in 2017 a few people). **Number 4.** "Nobody knows if Russia interfered with the election" (unless you count everybody). **Number 3.** "With the exception of the late, great Abraham Lincoln, I can be more presidential than any president that's ever held this office." (I know that's an opinion, but we all know Larry the Cable Guy would be more Presidential than Trump's utterly embarrassing, joke of a Presidency). **Number 2.** "We are going to repeal, and replace Obamacare, quickly, easily, on day one." (The President and the GOP has relentlessly attempted to repeal Obamacare. Republicans have made over 70 failed attempts). (Mostly prior to the Trump Presidency). **Number 1. "Fake News!!!!"** (Every scandal, every lie, it's all made up according to Donald. President Trump's cult followers are only all too happy to fall in line, and believe him, even when they heard or seen it for themselves.) **Bonus-** "Barack Obama was working with the head of a Muslim drug cartel. They have them, they don't tell you, but I assure you they do, and they are even bigger than the Mexican cartels. Barack made millions while he was President, he did, and I have proof, and I will show everyone along with his real birth certificate very soon." (Okay, he didn't actually say that.........Yet).

Trump consistently spoke during his campaign about how he was going to "drain the swamp" and like most anything that comes out of Trump's mouth, it is complete bullshit. Washington lobbyists who are the epitome of the swamp are doing as well or better than ever. According to statista.com, $3.37 billion were spent lobbying in 2017. That's right, $3.37 billion, with the influential NRA spending $5.1 million making sure assault rifles are readily available to anyone who would like to have a mass shooting of their own under their belt. The team President Trump assembled to advise him with his tax reform plan, and who are or were in key positions in the Trump White House, include former Goldman Sachs executives Steve Mnunchin, Gary Cohen, Dina Powell and Steve Bannon. Steve Bannon was banished, and I would imagine is sitting in his basement, not having showered in months, rubbing an AR-15 while plotting his revenge. Gary Cohen resigned as Director of the National Economic Council. Top national security adviser Dina Powell resigned, and returned to the open arms of Goldman Sachs as a partner in the Investment Banking Division while Trump defender, and Chief Economic Adviser Steve Mnunchin remains in the swamp, swimming around with the Donald. The biggest joke of all when it comes to doing the exact opposite of draining the swamp is the head of the EPA, Swamp King, Scott Pruitt. This guy is a walking nightmare for both our tax dollars, and the environment. In his life as an asshole prior to being put on as the head of the EPA, Pruitt consistently, and loudly called for the elimination of the agency he now heads. In a 2015 Fox Fake News interview, Pruitt stated the "environment would be just fine without the EPA."

Trump knew that in Pruitt he would get the pro-pollution, pro-business, anti-environmental protection person he wanted to undue any pesky laws that limit corporations from polluting our earth. As Oklahoma's attorney general that jackass, Scott Pruitt, sued the EPA 13 times. Yeah that's the guy we need to head our EPA. More than likely this isn't actually Trump's fault. It honestly could be as simple as no one actually told Trump what the letters "EPA" even stand for. Knowledge is the key to solving any problem, and when someone in charge lacks in-depth knowledge on any, and all subjects he is left to be guided by his greedy and selfish nature. According to the watchdog group American Oversight, Mr. Pruitt has, or is attempting to weaken, or eliminate many environmental protections. Pruitt vacated the planned ban of neurotoxic agriculture pesticide, "chlorpyrifos," which causes brain damage in children. Pruitt rolled back the Clean Power Plan to reduce pollution from coal fired power plants. We all know how Trump loves coal. Pruitt's campaigns, and political organizations received contributions from Clean Power Plan opponents including $25,000 from the coal company Murray Energy. Mr. Pruitt directed staff to scrub decades of climate change date from the EPA website, and got rid of any independent scientific advisors because "Science" is no friend to Mr. Pruitt's EPA.

In protest, and defiance to Mr. Pruitt, more than 700 EPA staff members have since left the agency they once worked for. Lastly, Swamp King Scott Pruitt's money, and pay for play scandals are almost as much of a daily story as Trump's marital affairs. Pruitt has spent millions of dollars on a 20 member, full time security staff detail that is more than three times the size of his predecessor's part-time security team. Swamp King, Scott Pruitt spends $43,000 for a soundproof booth. Mr. Pruitt also authorized large raises for two close aides, and to this day it does not seem Mr. Pruitt has followed through on his promise to rescind the raises. Mr. Pruitt, along with his security flies first class, and has used both private planes, and military jets to travel. Mr. Pruitt lived in an expensive Capitol Hill condo owned by a health care lobbyist, only while Mr. Pruitt stayed there it wasn't very expensive as he paid far, far less than the fair market price. Mr. Pruitt used his expensive security detail on trips to Disneyland, the Rose Bowl and Italy. Scott "the Swamp King" Pruitt travels around first class like he's a real king, and he is. Mr. Pruitt is definitely the Swamp King, congratulations Mr. Pruitt, and congratulations President Trump on another bullshit, un-kept promise. There are many other swamp creatures swimming around in the Trump administration. Urban Development Secretary and Professional Sleep Walker Ben Carson got himself into a

35

little hot water after attempting to buy a dining set for $31,000. Like most married men, Ben originally tried to blame his wife, but internal agency e-mails showed both himself, and his wife were aware and helped in selecting the furniture. I'm not sure if the entire White House is in rough shape or not, but 23 agencies have spent considerable amounts of money on renovations. Mr. Tom Price who was President Trump's first Secretary of Health and Human Services was fired in just over a half a year of service after apparently spending approximately $1 million in federal funds on private jet travel. It seems Trump's entire administration treats the government, and our tax dollars like we are their wealthy father, and they are our spoiled rich brats. Creepy Secretary Steve Mnunchin spent over $800,000 on seven flights he took using military aircraft. "Dad, I'm going to have Captain Frost fly me in one of the military planes. You know how I hate people." I think I'm starting to understand why Trump makes up these names for people. It's kind of fun; Swamp King Scott Pruitt, Creepy Steve Mnunchin, Sleep Walking Ben Carson.

Trump won poor, uneducated, white voters big, and it will be interesting if the policies that Trump, and GOP are putting in place which will clearly hurt his rural voters will end up hurting him. I've found facts mean little to the Trump voter so I'm not sure it will. President Trump can implement policies, and then just blame Obama, and they will probably believe him. Trump understands it's not what he does, but it's the feelings he creates by the things he says.

36

The only reason that thinking may get Trump in trouble this time is because they will have a feeling of hunger in their bellies. In the last election those voters listened to their feelings, now in order for Trump to win their votes they may have to listen to their heads, and not their hearts. Which one will win out? President Trump has started a bit of a trade war which could bring about tariffs on our exporting U.S. crops. China would put tariffs on pork, tobacco, and soybeans. Planned cuts in agricultural subsidies (Which, depending on how that would look I could be in favor of). What I would not be in favor of is cuts to food stamps, and work requirements which would hurt food stamp recipients who live in rural areas. I think many white Trump voters assume its lazy minorities who are stealing all the money from good, working, white people. Sorry Trumpsters, but working class whites make up the largest block of government funded poverty-reduction programs. Over 6 million whites benefit from government safety net programs, while African Americans represent just under 3 million, Hispanics about 2.5 million and "Other" representing about 700,000. Whites receive about 36% of all food stamps, African Americans about 26%, Hispanics about 17%. The remaining goes to "other" or "unknown." The extremely costly Medicaid program has over 40% of the benefactors being white, a little less than 20% being black, about 17% Hispanic and the rest coming from my favorite and the sometimes used by yours truly category of "Other." Okay, since this isn't Fox Fake News I'm going to shed a little light on those numbers here, and make some white people feel better. They say numbers don't lie, but they certainly can bend the truth, or at least be put out in a way that doesn't tell the whole truth. The Census Bureau measures who the recipients are of six government programs which include Medicaid, food stamps, housing assistance, supplemental Security Income (SSI), Temporary Assistance for Needy Families (TANF) and General Assistance. 42% of African Americans received at least one of these benefits, 36% of Hispanics, 18% of Asians/Pacific Islanders and 13% of non-Hispanic Whites. There are many factors as to why African Americans have the highest poverty rate, but I will write more about that in my brief section about race.

One of Trump's worst nominations was his nomination of an angry leprechaun named Jeff Sessions. The Attorney General is hell bent, with God on his side, at continuing, and enhancing the government's war on drugs. Sessions overturned the DOJ's policy instructing prosecutors not to specify drug amounts when filing charges against low level, non-violent offenders. Sessions would like to go after marijuana growers, and distributors in states where it is legal, thus flexing the federal government's power over state rights. Now this little angry leprechaun is tearing families apart, and separating children from their parents as they enter the country illegally or even in cases where they enter legally seeking asylum. Sessions gleefully stood before the cameras, and used the bible for justification for this Trump administration policy. Isn't it strange how those who proclaim to love Jesus the most act in the complete opposite manner Jesus acted? Trump is shamefully using children as bargaining chips to try and get financing for his border wall from the Democrats. Wait, I thought Mexico was paying for that?? Trump seems to be happy with Sessions at the moment, but we all know like any Trump marriage, it won't last. Hopefully Trump's disdain for Sessions over his handling of the Russia probe will motivate Trump even more to possibly legalize marijuana at the federal level. The legalization is inevitable anyway, and it's not just because public opinion is for the legalization of marijuana. In the end the thing that will push the legalization of marijuana over the top is corporations getting involved, and spreading the money around to buy the right politicians. The good news is Trump dislikes Sessions, and regrets nominating him as his AG in the first place, so maybe he will fire him after all. Feel free to call Mr. Sessions an "Angry Leprechaun" Mr. President.

I think I could keep going on and on about many of the things wrong with President Trump. I think as a country nothing surprises us anymore as to what we see Trump do, hear Trump say, or read Trump tweet. The problem is too much of the country loves it. We have an "us versus them" dynamic that is impossible to get out of now. Trump supporters are so entrenched on that side of things a fact is completely unrecognizable to them. It's become personal to Trump's supporters. Any criticism of Trump is a criticism of them personally. So what do we do?

Conclusion

About 25% of the country supports Trump no matter
what. There is also going to be a small percentage of the
country that is going to vote Republican because they are
easily fooled, and or distracted by the social issues which
they are aligned with on the Republican side. There is also
another small percentage that is aligned with the Republican
Party, and traditionally that's who they vote for no matter
what. Oh, and of course many, extremely wealthy
individuals.

Then we have a percentage of the country that is going to
vote with or for the Democratic Party. Approximately 48%
of all registered voters identify as Democrats or at least lean
Democratic compared to 44% of the country who identify as
Republicans. I won't get into the breakdown of race, gender,
etc. because I do not think that's necessary. The problem is
the perception that we can only have a viable candidate
from these two parties. They are both corrupt, and work
almost completely for corporation's interest. Are there
differences between the two parties? Sure, the Republicans
want to give corporations 99.9% of all the wealth in the
country while the Democrats want to only give the
corporations about 97% leaving us all with a few more
crumbs. I think the Trump administration is bringing out

the differences between the two parties more than ever. The Republicans are brutal, cold hearted, greedy, hate-filled bastards. The Democrats aren't much better, but the Democrats do understand they can't lock you out in the cold completely. The Democrats certainly have much more compassion for those without. The Democrats understand they need to throw you something, while the Republicans blatantly want it all! In the end though, the thing is, we are sick of choosing the lesser of two evils. That's partly what happened in the 2016 election. We wanted the best option, which was Bernie Sanders. When the Democratic Party stole that option for us, and tried to sell the argument of Hillary still being much better than Trump, we weren't buying it. I mean we were fairly certain that she would be the better option, but like I said earlier, fuck them. The whole corrupt two party system deserves one big fuck you from all of us. So many of us are so easily distracted by the bullshit social issues while they continually rob us all blind. The Democrats are every bit as complicit in the corrupt system itself as the Republicans are. What I mean by that is, the Democrats bow to corporate interests. The Democrats work for Wall Street, for the Military Industrial complex, for the prison industrial complex, for the pharmaceutical industry, and although they are the much lesser of the two evils we all deserve better. As a country we have to get out of the mindset that there are only two options.

I voted for Jill Stein in the 2016 election in hopes that she would garnish enough votes to start changing the two party narrative. Whose fault is it we cannot get a serious third party candidate? It is absolutely the national media's fault. We need to demand they give other candidates and parties equal coverage. The 2016 election produced the two most unpopular candidates in the history of our country. *In the history of our country*, and yet we couldn't find a viable third party candidate? In 1992 Ross Perot got 19% of the popular vote, but Mr. Perot had to fight tooth, and nail to be included into the debates. Since the 1992 debates not one third party candidate has been allowed to participate again. The media locks any other candidate out, refuses to give them any coverage, and when they do, the media never fails to keep reminding us all that the individual has no chance in hell of winning. Without adequate media coverage it's impossible for a third party candidate to break into the national consciousness. If Jill Stein was given proper coverage I have no doubt she could have competed with the two worst candidates in the history of the world. There was so much to dislike about both Hillary and Trump; a Jill Stein would have looked like a gift candidate. I'm not a Gary Johnson fan, because in all honesty he didn't seem too bright so that's why I'm not mentioning him as much as Jill Stein. Although, Mr. Johnson is for the legalization of marijuana, so there's one positive. Why not have a debate with 3 candidates? That needs to be the new norm. It would be the Republican candidate, the Democratic candidate, and whichever other Parties candidate is pulling the highest. If the media gave them equal coverage, and Americans became accustomed to having four choices then we wouldn't have a President Trump. I understand that sometimes we may get a President who much of the country dislikes, but with the exception of President Obama I don't recall having a choice for President where I felt, yes that should be our leader. The bottom line is we have to unite, get rid of the two party system that often resembles a one party system, and give the country more choices. Let's make America a true Democracy.

Afterthought

As I am writing this, Mr. Pruitt resigned. I don't think much will change with his departure as Andrew Wheeler will take over as acting administrator of the EPA. Mr. Wheeler has a similar mindset when it comes to climate change, big business, and reducing the size, and role of the EPA. However, maybe he will not live like a king on our tax dollars. Maybe by the time this is finished Trump will be indicted. Wishful thinking? We shall see.

As we all knew with the daily barrage of Trump related news we get it's almost impossible to keep up with so I've tried not to come back and comment, but yesterday's news was a little too big to ignore. Former Trump campaign manager Paul Manafort was found guilty of 8 counts. The news didn't end there. Trump's personal lawyer Michael Cohen plead guilty, and stated his crimes were committed in coordination with and at the direction of Donald Trump.

There is no doubt in my mind that Manafort will cooperate with the government now.(Mr. Manafort has cooperated). Trump is going down like Stormy Daniels in her famous movie "The Perfect Storm". Oh, wait, that was Mark Wahlberg, and George Clooney's movie. Stormy may have had a movie with the same title, but I don't know. As I stated earlier, as I am writing this book the news stories come in so fast it's impossible to keep up. Everything happening with President Trump's Supreme Court nominee Brett "I love beer" Kavanaugh is crazy. The opinions on if the extremely emotional judge Kavanough was lying or not is pretty much split along party lines. To me, he looks like an asshole, completely capable of doing exactly what he's accused of. That of course isn't enough to decide if he shouldn't be confirmed to the Supreme Court or not though so I listened carefully to both sides. After listening it was clear to me: One side did their best to tell the truth, and the other side tried to put on a show. Kavanough can't be trusted. Unfortunately, I think judge Kavanough will be confirmed. The Democrats don't have the numbers, and the Republicans don't have the morals. Republicans Susan Collins, and Jeff Flake are almost worse than the rest of those dirt bags. Both Collins and Flake stand in front of the camera, and pretend they have a conscience, and actually are going to do the right thing. However in the end both Collins, and Flake always stay true to their disgusting Republican Party. If Trump would have had to nominate another candidate, the candidate would have been a carbon copy so it wouldn't matter much. I know some people are concerned with him helping the criminal that is our President, but I think no matter who he nominated they would help him as well. In the end, they are all on the same team, and it's not ours.

Chapter-2

A Judicial Joke

America's criminal justice system is the ultimate hypocrisy of America. It is nothing more than an immoral jobs program that crushes individual's lives, and tears families apart. I didn't want to, but I guess I have no choice here, but to start with my own story. I was arrested for armed robbery along with my best friend Wared (Wadi) Abdellatif and Bobby Vitagliano. Myself and Wadi pled "not guilty", and went to trial while Bobby Vitagliano turned government witness, and testified against myself, and Wared Abdellatif. The federal government has a 98% conviction rate so the odds were stacked against us. I also had a couple of other charges stemming from the original charge including conspiracy to transport interstate commerce, and a witness tampering charge. The witness tampering charge was due to a stupid, inappropriate e-mail to an ex-girlfriend where I stated I wasn't going to jail for something I didn't do, and if she testified I was going to have to tell my lawyer everything I knew about her to discredit her. I should have never written the e-mail, but there was nothing I could do once it was sent. AOL, which was the e-mail of choice back then had an awesome "un-send" option. Unfortunately, I used yahoo mail, and when I realized I made a mistake, and I went to un-send the e-mail, unfortunately for me, that option was not available.

The trial was prosecuted by an immoral, piece of garbage prosecutor, Anthony Bruce. Mr. Bruce, like most prosecutors is only concerned with numbers. Mr. Bruce has come under fire many times for his unethical behavior. The judge in the case was a real piece of work as well, and I often wondered who was in charge of the trial, the judge or the prosecutor? That piece of garbage's name is Richard Arcara. Judge Arcara would often fall asleep during the trial, but since in the end the prosecutor was the one Judge Arcara was going to listen to, I guess Judge Arcara figured it didn't matter if he slept. It's my belief that all federal and state judges are pieces of garbage because they participate, and profit from our immoral criminal justice system. The trial itself had its ups and downs, but I felt pretty good about everything going into closing arguments. The night before, the jury came back with a verdict; a report was sent to the judge stating it was 11 to 1, but one person wouldn't change their mind, and needed to hear more evidence. I thought we were fucked, and not in the good way, but luckily I was wrong. Eleven of the jurors wanted to find both of us not guilty, with one juror wanting to find myself guilty of the witness tampering charge. Guilty of a witness tampering charge for a crime they found me not guilty of. It didn't even make sense, but in the e-mail I mentioned I would have to tell my lawyer my ex suffered from bi-polar disorder. Possibly this one juror may have suffered from mental illness herself, and she took what I wrote personally, and thus would not give in. The jury thought I would get a slap on the wrist, meaning probation. The guideline for the witness tampering charge carried a 10 to 16 month sentence. Even though for an e-mail a 10 to 16 month sentence would be excessive the sentence I received turned out to be much worse. In the federal system they can take acquitted conduct into account, and enhance your sentence outside your guideline range. In other words the judge can sentence you for conduct a jury of your peers found you Not Guilty of. When I tell my friends that 2/3rd's of my sentence was based on conduct I was found not guilty of, I can tell they almost don't believe me, or at least feel I have something wrong. They say, "No, they can't do that" well, one thing I've learned is "they" get to do anything they want. The rules only apply to the defendants. The judge, who is on the same team as the prosecutor, determines your guilt by a bullshit standard called a "preponderance of the evidence."

If you think the judge is a neutral party, you're a delusional fool. Your sentence is actually determined for the most part by the prosecutor, and a probation officer. The probation officer with the help of the prosecutor writes a pre-sentence report recommending a sentence to the judge. The guideline range they put me into taking into account my acquitted conduct was much higher than the 10-16 month sentence I should have received. I walked out of sentencing that day with a 48 month sentence.

I went to prison feeling confident I would win my

appeal. I remember meeting a guy in prison named Freddy. I don't remember his last name, but what I do remember was what he told me. Mr. Freddy said, you will never win because once they give you a number, they never let you go. I was still very naïve on what a joke our criminal justice system is, so I was certain I would win. As a part of the appeal we even obtained a letter from one of the jurors stating that all but one juror wanted to find me not guilty of the witness tampering charge, but they all compromised with that one juror to find me guilty even though they did not think I was guilty of the witness tampering. As a matter of fact the piece of shit FBI agent who got my ex to testify against me was the individual who did the real threatening. According to my ex, he was screaming at her, and told her she was going to be arrested and thrown in jail if she didn't sign a statement against me. Then the FBI agent wrote out the statement, and my ex-girlfriend signed it.

During sentencing my lawyer brought up this fact as it was also revealed at trial, and the scumbag, piece of shit judge played dumb and senile, and refused to even acknowledge what my lawyer was saying. Judge Richard Arcara kept repeating "What are you saying?" "What do mean?" he would never give an answer, and finally my lawyer became frustrated, and moved on from the issue. The appeal was filed, and I went to prison hoping to be home in about a year. I didn't know the appeals process was a complete farce. The news that I had lost my appeal was a difficult day. It was one of the two hardest days I had in

49

prison. My first difficult day came about one week into my sentence. My sister Marni was going to visit her husband Frank's family who lived fairly close to the prison. She brought her kids with her who I was very close with. I used to always stop by my sisters on the way home to see my nephew Austin, and my nieces Madison, Kelsi and Regan. Kelsi and Regan were both really young and were hanging on me as usual and happy as can be with really no idea I was in prison. As they left they were waiving at me not knowing this would be the last time I would see them for some time. I knew though and it broke my heart. In prison you're always alone, yet you're never alone, so it's tough to find a place where you can sort of grieve over a situation. I soon found something to pour myself into, and feel like I was able to fight back some. I started working on my own appeal called a 2255 Writ of Habeas Corpus. It's a civil appeal, and I truly loved doing the research, and putting together the appeal. I think I came up with 15 arguments, and a few were very promising. The judge has no time limit on when he has to look at and decide your appeal by, so it should not have shocked me that my scumbag judge waited until I was close to going home before denying my appeal. However, I did have a few issues that I appealed to the New York State Supreme Court and I actually won on a conflict of interest issue. With the court system being a farce though, the State court only remanded it back to Judge Arcara who obviously would never rule in my favor. So we went through the motions, and Judge Arcara denied the appeal, and the State Supreme Court did let him have that final decision.

I won't get into the details of the conflict of interest because it's not important. The issue that is important, and that should bother everyone is the fact my sentence was almost in entirety based on conduct that a jury of my peers found me not guilty of. In my Habeas Corpus appeal there was an interesting case before the United States Supreme Court that gave me hope. Actually, I was watching this particular case early on in my sentence, and when CNN reported how the case had been decided I almost started jumping up and down. I started making phone calls telling people based on this decision I should be going home ASAP. Again though, I was naïve, I had no idea what a farce the whole system is, and that God himself could not get you out of the federal system once you're in it. (Although, I'm agnostic, leaning toward an atheist anyway). The case I'm referring to was Blakely v. Washington. Ralph Howard Blakely kidnapped his estranged wife in an attempt to remarry her. Mr. Blakely's idea on winning his wife back wasn't exactly romantic. Mr. Blakely kidnapped his wife, and forced her into a wooden box in the back of his pickup truck all while making his 13 year old son follow behind in another car with the threat of having his mother shot if he did not. Mr. Blakely was originally charged with first-degree kidnapping, but in exchange for saving the state tax payers the unnecessary tax burden of going to trial, Mr. Blakely agreed to plead guilty to second degree kidnapping which carried a guideline range of 49 to 53 months in prison. The judge, finding that Blakely acted with "deliberate cruelty" imposed a sentence of 90 months. Blakely appealed his sentence as it violated his Sixth Amendment right to an impartial jury trial citing Apprendi v. New Jersey. Apprendi v. New Jersey was a Supreme Court case where the justices struck down state laws which allowed judges rather than juries to decide between life in prison or the death penalty. Blakely followed the same logic as Apprendi, and argued only a jury of his peers could find the extra sentencing decision, and that decision would have to be made under the "beyond a reasonable doubt" standard I think we all would want. The Supreme Court ruled, and applied their ruling in Apprendi in which it stated "Other than the fact of a prior conviction, any fact that increases the penalty for a crime beyond the prescribed statutory maximum must be submitted to a jury, and proved beyond a reasonable doubt." Justice Scalia went on to write the Apprendi rule ensures that "the judge's authority to sentence derives wholly from the jury's verdict. Without that restriction, the jury would not exercise the control that the Framers intended."

In case you're confused at all at this point, part of the factors being considered by the Justices are the guidelines, and the statutory maximum. The "statutory maximum for a particular crime may be 10 years, 20 years etc. An individual can be offered a deal to plead guilty and then the individual would be put in one of many guideline ranges. If

52

he admitted to certain factors he may fall into a 10 to 16 month guideline, or some other guideline range. In this particular case the facts that Blakely admitted to, put him into a guideline range of 49 to 53 months. At this point in time the guidelines were mandatory. Whether you were found guilty by a jury of your peers or you plead guilty, the facts of what you were found guilty of, or what you plead guilty to would put an individual into a particular guideline range. As a defendant, if you plead guilty, the biggest determining factor for you to make that decision is the guideline range you would fall into. Let's pretend you were charged in a crime which had a 10 year statutory maximum. If you thought the judge might impose a 9 ½ year sentence you may as well roll the dice and go to trial. However, if the state or federal government offers to put you into a 49 to 53 month guideline range in exchange for not going to trial, you would be motivated to take that deal. In Justice O'Connor's dissenting opinion the Justice feared or foresaw that in applying Apprendi to the sentencing guidelines, traditional sentencing factors would have to be charged in the indictment, and proved to a jury beyond a reasonable doubt. Yeah, no shit you asshole. That is exactly the way every American thinks this shit is being done in the first place!

Here's the problem with everyone being on the same team, and the defendant being out there by himself: You could have 19 charges against you with a small, insignificant charge thrown in with the more serious charges. The jury could then find you not guilty of 18 out of the 19 charges. That one charge may carry a 10 to 16 month sentence, but the judge could enhance the defendant's sentence for each charge, and as long as he stays under the 20 year statutory sentence he's fine. This exact scenario happened to a defendant while I was appealing my sentence. This poor guy was found not guilty on 18 out of his 19 charges. He ended up in the same 10 to 16 month guideline range as I did, but this poor bastard got a 19-year sentence! After I read about that case, I could not even complain about mine aloud any more. Nobody knows about this bullshit, and nobody cares about this bullshit until it happens to him or her or someone they love.

After the Blakey v. Washington decision; prosecutors, and judges throughout the country were in sheer panic mood. It was insane! The Supreme Court has lifetime appointees so sometimes many of the Justices are actually unaware of what's going on in the lower courts. What was going on was the lower courts had been fucking over defendants left and right with these enhancements. The enhancements are determined by the prosecutor, the pre-sentence report, which is written by a probation officer at the direction of the prosecutor, and the judge rubber stamps it. Now, just as I was excited at the prospect of having my sentence reduced to the 10 to 16 month sentence guideline range that the jury conviction should have put me into, as were many other defendants. Even more importantly, the corrupt criminal justice system needs to lock people up for long periods of time, and there are two things they depend upon: Prosecutors and judges count on enhancements not proved to a jury, and snitches. The government banks on giving defendants longer sentences, especially if you have the nerve to plead not guilty, and go to trial. The entire court system was literally going crazy! I'm sure many talks took place in private to let the Justices know what has been going on in the lower courts. Once the Supreme Court was made aware of the fact that thousands and thousands of people had been sentenced for crimes they were found not guilty of, nor plead guilty to the Supreme Court; then agreed to review two cases involving the constitutionality of the sentence enhancements under the federal guidelines. Due to the urgency of the many sweaty prosecutors, and judges the Supreme Court ordered the briefs in Booker to be submitted in September 2004, and oral arguments would take place on October 4th. The court's decision came out on January 12th 2005 even though the decision had been made behind closed doors months before by immoral prosecutors and judges pleading with the Justices to save their disgusting, corrupt system. The justice system, the country, and their jobs all depend upon it. So here's what these Supreme assholes did: The Supreme Court stated Booker was indeed correct. Mr. Booker's sixth amendment right to a jury trial had been violated. We won!!! Not so fast Mr. Booker! We are taking our time here in fucking with you, and then fucking you, call it foreplay if you will. Justice Stevens wrote "As the Blakely court found in Apprendi v. New Jersey, the 'statutory maximum' sentence a judge may impose solely on the basis of the facts reflected in the jury verdict or admitted by the defendant." There is no constitutional difference between the guidelines, and the statutory maximum. Be patient Mr. Blakely, we love foreplay. "Were the Guidelines merely advisory –recommending, but not requiring, the selection of particular sentences in response to differing sets of facts-their use would not implicate the Sixth Amendment. However, that is not the case. Title 18 U.S.C. A. 3553 (b) directs that a court "shall impose a sentence of the kind, and within the range." Established by the Guidelines, subject to departures in specific, limited cases. Because they are binding on all judges, this Court has consistently held that the Guidelines have the force and effect of laws. So listen Mr. Blakely with all this being said, I'm going to let Justice Breyer come in and have some fun with you as well. Don't worry though, Justice Breyer doesn't really like foreplay like I do. Justice Breyer is going to come in, and just fuck you. This will not feel good, but unfortunately it will be memorable in all the wrong ways.

Fuck away Justice...... "18 U.S.C. A.3553 (b) (1) which makes the Federal Sentencing Guidelines mandatory, is incompatible with today's Sixth Amendment "jury trial" holding and therefore must be severed and excised from the Sentencing Reform Act of 1984 (Act). Section 3742 €, which depends upon the Guidelines' mandatory nature, also must be severed and excised. So modified, the Act makes the Guidelines effectively advisory, requiring a sentencing court to consider Guidelines ranges, see 3553 (a) (4), but permitting it to tailor the sentence in light of the other statutory concerns." The Justices made it clear that courts should still sentence within the guidelines taking into account "circumstances for departure." In other words, the Justices knew what was taking place violated our constitutional rights; but once the Justices were informed of what was happening in the real world, the Justices changed the mandatory guidelines to advisory; eliminating the "shall" apply verbiage. Each Justice should be utterly ashamed of themselves. Every Congressman, and Senator should be ashamed of themselves as well.

For me, learning everything I learned was nothing less than heart breaking. If you hardly know anything of the constitution growing up, one of the phrases a person is usually familiar with is; the right to a trial by a jury of their peers. To learn that the government takes that basic constitutional right and spits on it, crushed me. I have no respect for judges, and most prosecutors. For prosecutors it's a numbers game. They rely on snitches, and they don't care what the snitch did as long as he or she gives them more people to lock up. Take Sammy "the Bull" Gravano who confessed to 19 murders, and was given a 5 year sentence just because he cooperated with the government. Some ninety prosecutors, and investigators wrote letters commending Gravano for his help. John Gleeson, the lead prosecutor in the John Gotti trial characterized Gravano as the most significant witness in the history of organized crime. I guess that's true considering Gravano's testimony helped imprison 36 of his former mob associates. The FBI's Jim Fox presented Gravano with an award reserved for agents who show uncommon valor which was a specially designed wristwatch with an American flag on its face. Judge Glasser believed Gravano had changed from a murdering gangster to a law and order advocate. I guess that didn't turn out to be the case because in 2000 Gravano was arrested, and indicted in an ecstasy ring that grossed $500,000.00 a week. One of the problems with rats is just like people who are tortured, you cannot depend on their testimony to be truthful. A rat will say anything to get out of trouble. Cooperating with the government is truly the only possible way to get a downward departure. When I was in prison you always knew if someone was a snitch because they would make up some bullshit story of why the judge was lenient on him. The problem for them was because they were a snitch they had no idea that you can't get less than the guidelines unless you cooperated.

Take rapper T.I. who was arrested on federal gun charges hours before he was set to perform on the BET Hip Hop Awards show. T.I. who is a convicted felon, bought three machine guns in a sting operation that involved one of his body guards who was a rat himself. Investigators found three more firearms in the car which T.I. drove to pick up the machine guns and silencers. Being a felon caught with any gun you are looking at an automatic five years, add the machine guns and the silencers - T.I. was looking at some serious time. Somehow, T.I. only received a sentence of a year and one day. The prosecutor stated T.I. was in a unique position to perform community service. The only community service T.I. performed was telling on everyone, and anyone he know anything about. I can't even imagine how many people T.I. snitched on in order to get the year-and-a-day sentence he received. I enjoy rap music, and I was a T.I. fan, but now I have to turn the station if I hear him rap. T.I. makes me sick, and I can't believe all the rappers out there who I'm sure have guys they grew up with doing serious time, and they still kick it with T.I. knowing he had to snitch to get that bullshit sentence. One of the CD's I listen to often is Biggie Duets, and T.I. raps a verse that goes "real niggers is doing their time, they ain't here, you commit the same crime come home the same year". Yeah you sure did you fucking rat. T.I. is still probably cooperating with the federal government, so if you're doing dirt in the ATL, watch out, because T.I. is taking notes. If you are wondering why I wrote about T.I. it's because the book is about hypocrisy, and here he is talking that tough shit, but when it came down to it, like most people he's soft as cotton.

Walking around the prison yard and staring at a 25 foot barbed wire fence isn't easy. You have to be mentally tough to take that. Being locked up does something to your soul, but as a man I always knew while I was walking around that I could do life if I had to. I certainly would not want to do life in prison, but the decision to rat on someone or to not rat on someone has to be made for yourself. Times

59

have changed. At one time, especially being Italian, if you were a rat you were ostracized from your community. I always think of the line in "A Bronx Tale" where Calogero says "I didn't rat dad, I didn't rat." Then, while thinking to himself he says "All I knew was, a rat was the lowest thing anyone could be in my neighborhood, and I didn't rat". It's not the way it is anymore though, therefore you have to not be a rat for yourself. For me, I could never rat someone out, and live with myself. When my father grew up as a young guy in Niagara Falls the mob was still big, and I think that was a value in the streets back then, and luckily for me he passed that value onto me.

I don't think very many policies have had more of a negative effect on poor communities, and especially on African Americans than the war on drugs. I'm trying to stay away from bombarding the reader here with a bunch of stats that end up not meaning much. When someone throws around too many stats it starts to skew the point they were actually trying to make. Emotion drives people to do something; facts and statistics unfortunately just don't have the effect they should. I will have to start out with some though, and then sprinkle a decent amount throughout, sorry. The American criminal justice system holds approximately 2.3 million people, with 1 out of every 5 people being incarcerated for a drug offense. To be honest I thought the number would be much higher. Well, actually it is; turns out if you get arrested for a drug offense as well as a more serious offense the crime is reported for the most serious offense only. According to the BOP (Bureau of Prisons) 46.2% of federal prisoners are incarcerated for drug offenses, and the number is probably higher in the State system.

As I wrote about earlier, I believe the criminal justice system is nothing more than an immoral jobs program. For every 100 people locked up there are approximately 35 jobs created; lock up another 100 people, 35 more jobs, lock up 100 more, 35 more jobs. Tying up individuals in the criminal justice system not only creates jobs, but it also takes millions out of the job market. I believe that's one of the reasons for the push to prosecute so many illegal immigrants. Currently just below 15,000 people are in federal prison for criminal convictions of violations of federal immigration laws. Federal Marshals hold almost another 15,000 immigrants in pretrial. Immigration and Customs Enforcement (ICE) civilly detain another 35,000 immigrants with that number steadily climbing under the Trump administration. These immigrants are housed in federally, or privately run immigration detention facilities, or in local jails under contract with ICE. It's not just immigrants that are coming across the border that we detain. Many people don't know this (Trump voice), but we actually go to other countries, and kidnap individuals suspected of drug offenses, and bring them to the U.S. and incarcerate them. The court system moves at the speed of a slow moving snail so what happens to these individuals is they sit in jail, and wait. Once these kidnapped foreign citizens have sat in jail for a year or two our government offers them a plea bargain of maybe 5 years. So this person then has a choice; do I go to what is probably going to be a fake trial, where I stand no chance of winning, and if I'm convicted I might go to prison for 20 years; or do I take the plea bargain for maybe something I didn't even do, but I can go home in a few years? The immigrants take what is seen as their only option, and pleed guilty. The U.S. government prefers not to grant bail. If an individual is sitting in prison doing time, it's counting toward their sentence so by the time they would go to trial they may have completed 30% or 40% of the time they are offered if they plead guilty. The United States has more individuals in pre-trial detention than most other countries even have in prison!

Currently the U.S. has nearly 550,000 thousand people waiting to either plea out or go to trial. While the United States only represents just under 5% of the world's population, we embarrassingly represent almost 25% of the world's prison population. The U.S. has the highest prison population rate at 716 per 100,000. China is the only country that even comes close to the U.S. on total prison population at approximately 1,650,000, but because they have such a huge population China doesn't even come close to us as far as their prison population rate goes. After China, the prison population totals around the world drop significantly. Italy has a prison population under 60,000 while Libya, and Lebanon combine for just over 12,000 prisoners.

Another point that indicates the prison system is in large part a jobs program is the system is set up to work as a revolving door leading individuals right back to prison shortly after they are released. I understand the need for pre-trial parole officers much more than post sentence served parole officers. Once you have served your time, the government should not be able to keep applying pressure, and watching your every move so they can lock you back up. Each year 626,000 individuals are released from prison. The problem is that large portions from the present year, along with those from a combined number of years where individuals are still on parole, end up going in and out of prison 10.6 million times per year. That stat comes from various ways people enter, and exit the prison doors. Some people, like myself, made bail, then another charge was brought by the prosecutor so they rearrested me, then the FBI agent, and the state trooper scooped me up for a third time in hopes the judge would revoke my bail. However, the judge let me stay out on house arrest. Myself, and others have to understand if I were black I more than likely would not have made bail at this point. First off, my parents, two of my sisters, and myself all put up our houses for bail. The bail amount was over a quarter million dollars in equity from the homes we had. How many people have access to that? In "Following the Money of Mass Incarceration" Peter Wagner, and Bernadette Rabuy give some fantastic insights on where some of our money is spent, and who benefits from keeping things just as they are. The authors write

"Almost half the money spent on running the correctional system goes to paying staff. This group is an influential lobby that sometimes prevents reforms, and whose influence is often protected even when prison populations drop." I remember a shirt that one of the ignorant, Trump-type of correctional officer wore while I was in prison: The shirt was a play on the movie "Field of Dreams" starring Kevin Costner, but it was a portrait of a prison and it stated "build it, and they will come." What an asshole, not Kevin Costner, he's awesome, I'm a big fan; the corrections officer, he's the asshole. Yet, he thinks only the prisoners are the pieces of garbage.

Wrongful convictions are a consistent problem in the criminal justice system. Often when an individual is wrongfully convicted, prosecutors and judges do everything they can not to admit they made a mistake. Furthermore, prosecutors usually fight the release of the person who was wrongfully convicted. What kind of immoral, cold hearted scumbag could take a person's freedom from them for years upon years, find out they did not commit the crime - yet not feel the need to get them out of prison ASAP!? What these immoral prosecutors often do is offer the wrongfully convicted individual an Alford plea. Take the case of James Owen and James Thompson, two individuals that were wrongly convicted of a 1987 rape, and murder. In 2006 DNA evidence from Semen found inside the victim proved the state indeed had the wrong men. Prosecutors, never willing to admit they were wrong, still said they had the right guys, and were not going to just let these two men out of prison where they were serving life sentences. The unwillingness of prosecutors to admit they were wrong, yet the fact that they knew they were wrong led the prosecutors to offer an Alford plea. An Alford plea offers an immediate release from prison with no retrial, and no risk of a new conviction. If the prosecutors honestly believed the men were guilty why would they offer such a deal? We all know they knew they were innocent, and it blows my mind how they can even sleep at night knowing they ruined these innocent men's lives. Mr. Thompson had enough, and took the Alford plea. I guess I can understand to an extent. Prison can mentally defeat a man, and the chance to be free again immediately was just too good to turn down for James Thompson. Plus Mr. Thompson was a weak snitch who actually testified against his "friend" James Owen. The reason I chose this sort of complex case where at one point there was a confession, and some evidence actually did suggest that Mr. Owens and/or Mr. Thompson were the right men, is because the police left out crucial evidence, and both the police and the prosecutor withheld details that could have led to the acquittal of Mr. Owens. In a way, fuck James Thompson because he's just as bad as the prosecutor. James Owens however would have none of it. I don't know Mr. Owens, but I feel his resolve, probably fueled by anger, and the need to show his family, his friends, his acquaintances, and everyone else what he said all along was always the truth. Mr. Owens had to wait 16 more months while that piece of garbage prosecutor hoped that he would cave in, and finally take that Alford plea. Just writing this makes me so angry because I saw the heart of these prosecutors, and how little they care about anything other than getting the conviction. Well, that degenerate should at minimum have to serve the 16 months he made Mr. Owens wait for no reason. What kind of individual would do that? Who in their right mind would do something so unscrupulous? Prosecutor Marvin Brave, that's who. I wish what he did was the exception but it isn't. All too often prosecutors withhold evidence, and in the rare times they get caught they usually offer the Alford plea so they can in part save face, and not admit their mistake. Also, if the defendant accepts the Alford plea then the defendant cannot sue. It's bad enough people spend years in prison for something they didn't do, but you don't think the wrongly convicted deserve some monetary compensation? We can't give them back their youth so the least we can do is give them some financial freedom.

Since 1980, 147 individuals who were on death row have been exonerated. Can you imagine how many innocent people we have killed? It's not as if once the state is presented with crucial facts to show the innocence of a defendant they help make sure justice is served. The state continually does the complete opposite. The United States was not always a leader in locking people up. In 1970 there were only approximately 200,000 Americans behind bars. It took the U.S. until 1990 to reach one million behind bars. The prison population started climbed steadily from the 1970s on though. Once we hit our first million in prison, we quickly doubled that in only ten years' time. I think it's disgusting that we have gotten to this point, and unless we can restart the Bernie revolution, I don't think we could ever have enough politicians with the moral fortitude to turn these insane numbers upside down. The recent election of Alexandria Ocasio-Cortez gives me some hope though.

Another reason for mass incarceration is that it's a continued form of segregation. African Americans make up 13% of the U.S. population, 40% of the U.S. prison population with 60% of prisoners being people of color. I'm not a conspiracy theorist, but our government has always backed policies that segregate African Americans, and being segregated makes finding success much more difficult. Some segregation types of legislative policies enacted by our government include "The National Housing Act of 1934" where the federal government allowed the Home Owners Loan Corporation to create discriminatory security maps where they would highlight minority neighborhoods in red, and then deny loans in these areas. The Federal Housing Administration furthered segregation by subsidizing builders to build entire suburbs where the houses were only sold to white families. The sales of homes excluded African American families on the basis that selling homes to black families would bring down home values. This maintained a system of housing African Americans away from the rest of society. In New York City for example 85% of the subdivisions built in the 1930s and 1940s had FHA restrictions for selling homes to African Americans.

It isn't that Roosevelt and his New Deal didn't try to help African Americans at all, but when these certain types of programs are created under the mindset of keeping black and white people separated from each other; that's what you get. "The Housing Act of 1937" is a great example of this. This act created approximately 160,000 public housing units for the poor where they placed all poor minorities together. I would think back then the Roosevelt administration thought they were doing wonderful things to help black America, but segregating the poor creates a cycle because that is what you see as you're growing up. In 1944, Roosevelt signed the "Servicemen Readjustment Act" or "the GI Bill." This bill gave education, training opportunities, loans for homes, and job finding assistance. Again, African Americans were discriminated against when they attempted to purchase a home in a white neighborhood. Banks usually would not loan to African Americans, and often realtors wouldn't even show homes in white neighborhoods to potential purchasers who were black. Home ownership in our country is really the easiest way to create any kind of wealth/worth. If you live in a home you purchased for 20 years then you have a good amount of equity. If you're paying rent for the same 20 years you have built up nothing except wealth for the landlord. Furthermore, if you were to die after the same 20 years of paying on a mortgage there would be a home to pass on to a child. Thus that lack of home ownership gave one part of the population some worth, while another part of the population contributed to the others worth in the form of rent. Those homes could have been passed down for generations, and when these FHA and GI loans were given out, African Americans could have afforded to buy a home. Nowadays, it's very difficult to purchase one of those homes in a comparable area. The good news is segregation is less today than it ever has been. Today almost 40% percent of African Americans live in the Suburbs. The benefits that come along with a move from a poor inner city to a suburb can't be over exaggerated; There are better schools, better homes, cleaner neighborhoods, less unemployment, more two parent families. If you see these positive things growing up then you expect nothing less for yourself, and your family.

The problem is the 60% of African Americans who are growing up in inner cities are subject to more policing, and if they make one mistake they are funneled into a system that is difficult to get out of. Prisons are built to put people in them, especially people of color. I believe it's much more of a jobs program, but in order to have that jobs program you need inmates, and where are you going to get those inmates from? From the suburbs? No way! Can you imagine if the jails were filled with young white males like they are young black males? I understand many people believe they are committing more crimes, and that's why they are being locked up at a much higher percentage, and it's not as if they are getting arrested for nothing. Okay, but the truth is many of the crimes involve the sale of drugs; blacks and whites sell and use drugs at about the same rate; about 12%. However, African Americans go to prison for those offenses at six times the rate of whites. I've been going back and forth debating myself; with the closing of the civil rights era, and with African Americans having some success in making political gains for themselves, did our government turn to incarceration as a new means to punish, segregate and subjugate African Americans? Or, did our government start with a few changes in policy, witnessed our incarceration rates rise, see the jobs that were being created, and felt this was a beautiful consequence, and one that must be continued. I tend to believe it was the latter. I think jobs were created; African Americans, and Hispanics were removed from the streets, and our government looked at it as a win-win.

With the exception of job creation, the costs of having the highest incarceration rates in the world are tremendously bad from every other point of view. Breaking down some of the financial costs of mass incarceration is sickening. With all levels of government combined we spend over 80 billion dollars a year on corrections. 80 billion dollars! Republicans!! Think how you can spend that money on dropping bombs on people around the globe, supporting corrupt regimes that brutalize their people, allow our corporations to rape their land, or giving it to our corporations who fund your campaigns (Democrats too). Wouldn't that be awesome for you? I understand your dilemma. What will you do with all those prisoners you release to society and all the jobs that would be lost? We could put them to work rebuilding our crumbling

70

infrastructure. I know, not exactly a new idea, but unfortunately one you really haven't taken to heart, and started either. I know markets for labor have demand, and supply curves just as there is a supply, and demand laws concerning the markets of goods. So in the end just get the people out of prison who shouldn't be there in the first place, and then we can go from there. We need more social workers, and drug councilors so maybe we could train people, and put them to work in those fields.

Probation officers should be social workers, helping former prisoners instead of adding stress to their already stressful return to the real world. For me, being on supervised release was a constant stress, and I would have gladly done another year in prison, and come out truly free instead of being under the governments thumb for four more years. 76% of people on probation violate their parole, and return to prison within five years. Do you honestly think the system isn't set up that way on purpose? They need that revolving door in, and out of prison. The constant monitoring of individuals on paper, and the payment of fines helps keep those prison doors open, and makes it near impossible to get yourself out of that cycle of poverty and prison, prison and poverty. When a city levies fines, and the individual is unable to pay it usually leads to an arrest. Some cities offer community service for people who can't afford to pay their fines, but many do not. Some defendants are unable to pay a fine because they are homeless or have mental health issues, and the courts rarely ask the defendant why he or she cannot pay their fine. Why would they? Judges understand how the system works, and the poor are the easiest victims. The poor also have the least means to defend themselves. If you are poor, you're going to feel as if this cycle will never end, and you will never get out. Justice is only for the rich. Take the unethical, disgusting human being, Dr. James Corasanti. This dirt bag was drunk, texting his then mistress when he hit and killed 18 year old Alix Rice. The impact of Corasanti's BMW snapped the bones of both Rice's lower legs, broke ribs, lacerated her cerebellum, and caused neck injuries among other injuries which resulted in her painful death. Corasanti knew he hit her. Alix Rice's body was hit so hard she flew 167 feet. A witness heard Rice getting hit because the sound was so loud. Film footage from near Corasanti's home shows Corasanti rushing out of his house almost 30 minutes after the accident. Where to? His attorneys. Corasanti's wife was with him. Neither Dr. Corasanti nor his wife called 911 after parking the car in their garage and seeing the extensive damage, along with the blood and tissue. Somehow the jury acquitted the good doctor. If Dr. Corasanti were a poor African American, a poor Hispanic, oh hell, a poor anyone, they would have been convicted without a doubt. Justice is only for the rich. The rich are getting richer in many ways, but also by way of the prison industrial complex. The crime-control industry in general is a huge money maker and as usual on the backs of the poor. Prisons, and crime prevention industries are publicly funded. It's the construction industry, the real estate industry, the technology industry, the pharmaceutical industry. Plus prisons produce a massive slave labor force. Companies such as McDonald's purchase goods produced in jails such as plastic cutlery, containers, and have uniforms sewn in prisons. Walmart uses prison labor to strip UPC barcodes and serial numbers from Walmart products so they can be re-sold to after-market retailers. Victoria's Secret isn't what you thought it was; they actually use female inmates in South Carolina to sew undergarments and casual wear. AT&T used inmates to work their call centers! These companies make huge profits, and could pay American workers a decent wage, instead they are increasing their profits by taking advantage of the prison slave labor system. Here are a few other notable companies that benefit from prison slave labor; Bayer, Chevron, Koch Industries, Motorola, Pfizer, Procter & Gamble and Microsoft!

The use of a prison labor force isn't the only way private industries cash in on the prison industrial complex; Companies produce, and sell everything from prison jumpsuites, food trays, mattresses, massive amounts of shitty, expired food, phone services, healthcare, and honestly too many other items to bother listing. All these companies benefit from having large prison populations, and all are extremely happy that America is not the land of the free, but rather the land of lock um up. Charging inmates exorbitant rates for making phone calls is criminal in itself. It costs inmates and their families just under $4.00 dollars for a 15 minute call. If the inmate makes a collect call the rates are even worse. Global Tel Link charges the insane rate of $1.13 per minute for collect calls. Most inmates and their family members are not exactly rich, and this puts severe strain on families just to try and stay in touch with their loved one. I'm all for company's making money, but when Global Tel Link is able to make over 500 million dollars annually operating in state and federal prisons, the government should be able to step in and set the rates so everyone

73

benefits. Wouldn't 100 million dollars a year be pretty good? If inmates' families paid .23 cents a minute that would put Global Tel Link at slightly over 100 million dollars a year. 100 million a year sounds awesome to me, but corporations + politicians = Greed. That equation is the reason prison populations won't decrease. That equation is the reason we are an empire, and need our military industrial complex. That equation is the reason we can't get corruption out of politics. That equation rules our world, and always will, unless we all ban together to say enough is enough.

Conclusion

We need a new massive civil rights movement. We all have to demand political change. We have already seen the solution will not come through the courts, so it has to come through our representatives. "Our" Representatives. I know most of the country believes we have to do something to get our incarceration rates down. I know most of the country believes a defendant should only be sentenced on what he or she either plead guilty to or was found guilty of. So why are we not demanding this take place? Call your state Senator. Demand change. Call again. Organize protests. Mandatory sentencing statutes have to end, and the larger statute associated with a particular crime needs to be narrowed. This way it leaves judges the ability to adjust sentences, and make sure the sentence fits the crime committed. If we narrow the statutes on the whole we won't see cases where one defendant gets 15 years in Alabama for the same crime a defendant in New York received a one year sentence for.

Any changes in laws need to be made retroactive. We have so many individuals who sold drugs in their early 20s, who are now in their 40s or 50s and are still in prison. The sentences they received were way too long in the first place. Education is the key to prisoners leaving prison better men, and woman. I would not want to see free college education for prisoners because I know the backlash would be too great, and I understand. I have $80,000 in student loans so I understand why individuals would be upset if someone in prison is able to get a free education. Just so we are clear, I wouldn't be angry, but I can understand where many would. Therefore we should focus on trades. Trades are a great fit anyway because they will ensure prisoners are hirable right out of prison.

Parole officers should be used to help prisoners in their return to society. Help give former inmates the tools, and resources they need to make sure they don't return to prison. I'm a huge believer in community policing. We need mentorships with police officers, and inner city youth. We need more police athletic leagues sponsoring boxing, and basketball leagues. I know some fantastic police officers who would be great at leading these types of efforts. Well, not personally, but I've heard they exist. (Just kidding Tony and Scott) (Two family members who are fantastic people, and I'm sure fantastic police officers as well) I often criticize Judges and Prosecutors, but I know some of them are fantastic people who are often handcuffed and unable to act in the way they would wish or that is just. My friend and fellow Pittsburgh Steeler fan John Andrews is one of the nicest guys I know and he is an Assistant District Attorney which gives me hope there are many more who are equally kind, caring, good hearted individuals. If you want to get involved tomorrow start by calling your representatives.....often! See what or if the PAL (Police Athletic League) is sponsoring in your community, and work with them on a project that will benefit the community, and their attitudes toward police.

The following is the letter to Judge Arcara from one of the jurors in my trial:

Dear Judge Arcara,

I am writing this letter in support of James Ventry who was found guilty of witness tampering by the jury of which I served. When I was selected to be a jury member, it was a stressful and scary time for me. I felt unqualified to be making a judgment that could greatly alter the lives of two young men. After listening to almost three weeks of testimony from alleged victims, supposed friends and ex-girlfriends-some of which were perjurers-we as jurors had to make some kind of sense of this information to come to a unanimous decision. Testimonies regarding bookmaking, gambling, home invasions, guns, and "mob" bosses haunted our minds. This subject matter was entirely out of the realm of reality for many of us jurors. To put it simply-we couldn't relate! It was more like a comedy version of the Soprano's. Maybe it's pure ignorance on my part, but how could any of us make a judgment when these peopled lived entirely different kinds of lives. Well thank God for laws. My very first impression was that these two men probably committed these alleged crimes or this case wouldn't be in federal court to begin with. I thought "Why would the United States waste time and money if they weren't certain they could get a conviction". As testimonies came to an end, I was confused as ever and was looking forward to hearing what the other juror's impressions were. You then spent hours reading us the laws and giving us guidelines to correctly come to a unanimous decision. The words "Beyond a reasonable doubt" hung over all our heads as we returned to the deliberation room. The evidence presented was so dramatically opposed that we all agreed the only believable testimonies came from a Ford dealer, a man who made store signs and the victim of the home invasion. In fact, 11 out of 12 of us had reasonable doubt and we agreed we had to deliver a verdict of "not guilty" due to lack of evidence. For one and half days we tried to reason with one juror who was unreasonable.. We argued collectively that the decisions couldn't be feelings, that we had to go by the guidelines of the law and if her basis for conviction was based on "A gut feeling" that in fact was not evidence but doubt! With the Thanksgiving holiday days away, angry employers becoming less patient, temperatures "heating up" in the deliberating room and mostly, the embarrassment of causing a mistrial, we compromised with one juror to acquit the men on the first four charges and convict Mr. Ventry on the last one. After the verdict was read and each of us stood before you and the court to verify our own verdicts, I couldn't help but feel sad and guilty that I compromised my own beliefs by "cutting a deal" with a person who was just plain ignorant.

After the trial was over and I was able to discuss the case, I found out that a lot of people I know knew of the case and some worked in the same school district as Mr. Ventry. They told me how much he is loved and respected by students, parent, faculty, and the school board. Here is a guy who loves to teach and is an effective teacher. Mr. Ventry is clearly an asset to our society and has worked very hard to accomplish the goals needed to become a positive role model for our children. The fact that he is making a difference right now is what counts. Great teachers are few and far between, I would be grateful to have him teach my own children and make a difference in their lives, especially in the uncertain society we live in now. I am asking you to please overturn the witness tampering charge Mr. Ventry's January 27, 2003 sentencing and get this young man back in the classroom where he belongs!

Respectfully yours,

Name Removed for privacy purposes

Chapter 3

Military Industrial Complex, and American Imperialism

Much like the prison industrial complex, the military industrial complex is another immoral jobs program, and even more of a money making machine for corporations. The United States has been in a war time economy since the end of World War II. For the U.S., WWII was the best thing that ever happened for its economy and power throughout the world. The valuable lesson we learned is producing military goods was good for our corporations, and good for our country. Our leaders began following an endless policy of military engagement throughout the world using the threat of communism as its justification. After WWII, Military spending slowed down for a couple years, but then with the start of the Korean War in 1950 military spending increased to approximately 15% of our GDP. The U.S. has remained war ready or at war, so our spending on our armed forces has always been high, but as far as it relates to our GDP it has fluctuated throughout the years. The cost of U.S. Military spending during the entire Cold War era (1947-1991) was 13.1 trillion dollars, with an average of almost 300 billion dollars annually. 13.1 trillion is an almost incomprehensible number for most of us, but it actually pales in comparison to spending under the War on Terror considering the Cold War era spending took place over almost five decades.

Cold War spending also includes The Korean War, and the Vietnam War. The Cold War victory left our government in search of another reason to keep our military spending at such high levels. The War on Terror is a perfect fit because it can use fear to fight an enemy that can be both real and imagined. The Center for Strategic & International Studies estimates the Afghanistan and Iraq wars are more than five times more costly than the Korean War, and 2.5 times more expensive than the Vietnam War. The Congressional Research Service (CRS) puts the total cost of the Afghanistan and Iraq wars at 1.6 trillion, but that fails to take into account future costs such as medical care for injured military personnel. There have been many studies into the true costs for those wars with most putting the costs somewhere between 4 and 6 trillion dollars. According to the Watson Institute International & Public Affairs, the costs of post September 11, 2001 Wars, Veterans Care, and Homeland Security total 5.6 trillion dollars. The real issue is our politicians have no desire to curtail our military spending in any way. Cutting military spending is a difficult political move for multiple reasons. First off, almost no one wants to propose cuts to our military, and appear to make our country weaker or at least open themselves up to criticism from someone from the opposite political party. Second, just like the criminal justice system, the military industrial complex is a jobs program on many fronts; both home and abroad.

Our top military contractors employ thousands of individuals, make huge sums of money, depend upon global

U.S. intervention, and contribute to political campaigns to ensure all remains as is. The top five defense contractors in the United States are Lockheed Martin, The Boeing Company, Raytheon Company, General Dynamics Corporation, and the Northrop Grumman Corporation. There are many others who also make billions including General Electric who earns approximately 3.5 billion dollars a year. That's probably a little more than they earn selling stoves and refrigerators. Lockheed Martin employees 126,000 people, and is headquartered in Fort Worth, Texas. Lockheed Martin Aeronautics is based in Marietta, Georgia, and Palmdale, California. Lockheed Martin, like other defense contractors, do not want to see any spending cuts that might diminish their profits. Also, when cuts are proposed, these companies threaten to lay off hundreds of their employees. Yet year after year these companies make record profits. In April 2018, Lockheed Martin reported their first quarter 2018 net sales which were 11.6 billion dollars. When these companies threaten to lay off American workers it's more than greedy, it's treasonous. Why aren't these companies who make billions off of our tax dollars expected to show loyalty to those who make them wealthy? Even if there were military budget cuts that lowered defense contractors profits, don't they owe it to their workers to keep them employed? I think that goes for all corporations. If they are losing money, that's one thing, but to maximize shareholder profits at the expense of their employees is inexcusable.

The top 8 defense contractors employ almost 900,000 people, and those contractors use the threat of layoffs every time any cuts to defense spending are proposed. In 2016 Lockheed Martin spent 13.6 million dollars lobbying, but don't worry, lobbying pays handsome returns. In that same year, Lockheed Martin had 47.2 billion dollars in net sales, and 3.8 billion dollars or $12.38 per share in net earnings. I think when we see these huge numbers the sums almost lose their meaning. So, to put it in perspective, if you have a pretty decent job, and after taxes you clear $800.00 a week, it would only take you **four million, seven hundred and fifty thousand weeks** to equal the net earnings Lockheed Martin achieved in 2016. You may want to pack a lunch. All big companies are spending big money making sure their voices are heard, and their money is well spent. Northrop Grumman spent 12 million lobbying. Boeing spent 17 million in lobbying. Boeing's lobbying paid off nicely in 2016 receiving 148 government subsidies totaling over 13 billion dollars. Yet today I saw a meme about limiting what foods someone can buy with their food stamps.

It's crazy how we never seem to care about corporate welfare, but when it's grandma or a single mother, fuck them. The obvious jobs program are the soldiers themselves. According to the Department of Defense, as of January 31st 2018, 1.4 million individuals were serving in the United States armed forces. In Germany we still have 35,000 active-duty troops stationed there. I know we didn't find Hitler's body but come on, I promise he's not coming back. In Japan, the United States has slightly more troops than in Germany with the total being just under 40,000, followed by South Korea at almost 24,000. Combined the U.S. has just under 200,000 troops in a total of 177 countries. If you're unaware or even if you somewhat know, your mind should be blown away by this fact. We have right around 800 military bases in 177 countries. Our government has no desire to eliminate these military jobs, and bring many unskilled workers back to U.S. soil where they would be looking for menial work. Also, the U.S. needs our troops spread across the globe. Why? In part, as previously mentioned, it's a jobs program, and the other reason the U.S. has a global empire is to ensure our corporations protection, their rights to steal other countries natural resources, and sell their goods and services. I'm not saying all the benefits we receive are a bad thing. We have a great, mutually beneficial relationship with the European Union which is our largest trade partner. We limit Russian influence, and share intelligence. NATO would, and does help to defend the United States if or when it were attacked. European allies also cover 34% of the U.S. basing costs, which totals 2.5 billion dollars annually. In Northeast Asia, the United States looks to counter Chinese influence, and support South Korea, and Japan. Our relationship seems to change daily with North Korea due to the erratic leadership of both North Korea's President Kim Jong-Un, and the United States wannabe Dictator, Donald Trump. In Southeast Asia, the U.S. military protects our trade interests in the South China Sea, which totals about 1.2 trillion dollars in trade with the United States. Due to American oil dependency, U.S. military presence in the Middle East is extremely beneficial to the United States.

Our constant presence in the Middle East both creates terrorists, and keeps the fight against terrorism off of American soil. I think an unforeseen consequence of increased U.S. fighting in the Middle East is an increase in home grown terrorists. Many individuals who are sympathetic to certain Middle Eastern countries see America's role in the Middle East as an anti-Muslim role. I guess keeping the fight against terrorism in the Middle East is a good thing for the most part though, at least for America. The United States drops bombs, creates poverty, death, and devastation. The question of "why do they hate us" has been asked and answered a million times. We know why they hate us. You can debate on whether their responses range from rational to irrational, but our government understands there is going to be a response. We need a response, otherwise we can't keep dropping bombs, and then we would need a 1980s type Cold War again in order to keep giving money to Boeing, and the likes. Although, I guess when you spend the money these corporations spend lobbying, you don't have to have much of a justification. In 1983, Ronald Reagan came up with the Star Wars initiative (not to be confused with the Star Wars movies). The Strategic Defense Initiative System was a defense against an intercontinental ballistic missile attack. Now, 35 years later President Trump is taking that to another level with his ridiculous "Space Force". Oh, Trump supporters love Space Force. One illiterate Trump supporter expressed the reason he liked the idea of Space Force, "because it sounds fucking cool man." Oh Lord, please help us. Our Military already spends about 15 billion per year on space defense items such as military communications satellites, but I'm sure the Donald has much cooler things in mind. Since 1983, over 55 billion dollars has been spent protecting the U.S. against missiles launched by the then

Soviets, and now the worry is Iran, and North Korea. Oh, and I think Trump mentioned those sneaky Canadians as well. I love Canada by the way. I spent years there boxing at the Shamrock Boxing Club. Some of the best guys, and fighters I've ever met came out of the gym. Okay, sorry, back on point. The truth is the "War on Terror" keeps the excuse for a Military Industrial Complex to keep thriving, and if somehow the war of terror ended like the Cold War did something else would be created to take its place.

Beyond our military, we are in the business of covert operations, involving un-American acts such as overthrowing democratically elected leaders, invasions, and assassinassions. The Central Intelligence Agency (CIA) and the National Security Agency (NSA) do the U.S.'s dirty work in these areas. A lesser known agency, the Defense Intelligence Agency (DIA) works to collect, and analyze data. They may be of service at times to the CIA, and the NSA, but in general they seem more defensive than offensive. If Donald Trump colluded with Russia then there is a big problem, but as far as what Russia did - people from the left need to get a grip. Russia did exactly what they are supposed to be trying to do. Are we up in arms because they were successful? We go so far beyond what Russia did that it's disgusting for people here to act so appalled. The NSA spies both at home and abroad. The NSA also creates computer viruses to cause dismay to our enemy's computer systems. In 2013, Edward Snowden revealed that the NSA was actually spying on American citizens, and not just foreign countries. The first bombshell showed Verizon had been providing its customers phone records to the NSA. The NSA, as we would all expect, spies on leaders of other countries. I'm not sure why this was such a shock, other than perhaps some of the taps may have been to the leaders personal phones. Snowden's leaks revealed a number of other insights into what the NSA is secretly doing, including intercepting some 200 million text messages (but shame on Russia for their fake news stories). Honestly, it's "shame on President Obama for not pardoning Mr. Snowden", and for his administrations crackdown, and punishment of fellow whistleblowers.

No other country interferes in other countries politics more than the United States of America. The United States has such a long history of meddling in other countries elections, you could say it's in our DNA. This was actually confirmed in a recent Ancestry.com investigation. Okay, maybe not, but Carnegie Mellon University's Dov Levin found the U.S. interfered in elections over 80 times! Some countries where the U.S. interfered are Guatemala, Brazil, El Salvador, Haiti, Panama, Israel, Lebanon, Iran, Greece, Italy, Malta, Slovakia, Romania, Bulgaria, Albania, Sri Lanka, Philippines, South Vietnam, and Japan. Countries like Iraq aren't included in this list, perhaps an illegal invasion of a foreign country is in a whole other category. The first attempt, and success the CIA experienced in election tampering came in 1948 when it gave funds and support to the Christian Democrats in Italy to beat the pro-Russian Socialist Democrats. I guess that first taste was like when Chris Rock's character "Pookie" got his first taste of crack cocaine in New Jack City. Hopefully Pookie got better because the U.S. is still a raging addict. Again, it's the brainwashing that we have gone through that makes us believe it's okay for the United States to be involved in regime change, but no other country has the right. Almost every U.S. President since Roosevelt has been involved in successful or unsuccessful regime change attempts. When the U.S. overthrows a democratically elected leader it should bother us all. The U.S. loves democracy, no?? I hate the hypocrisy of America.

I don't think it's necessary to cover each immoral act, but a few are worth writing about, and one that I've read quite a bit about, and I found disturbing because of the brutal results was the overthrow and murder of freedom fighter Patrice Lumumba in the Congo. Lumumba was the first Prime Minister of the Congo, formerly the Belgium Congo. Lumumba first turned to the U.S. and the United Nations in hopes of having a smooth transition, and quelling those who were violently fighting for power. The problem was Lumumba was a leader who wanted to use his nation's resources for the betterment of his people, and not the foreign corporations of Belgium, and the United States. Ultimately, Lumumba turned to the Soviet Union, and democratically elected or not that was his final nail in his own coffin. President Eisenhower floated around the idea to the CIA of poisoning Lumumba, but in the end the CIA supplied weapons and funds to his enemies who eventually murdered Lumumba by firing squad. Sadly for the Congo, the new leader who emerged was the U.S. backed brutal dictatorship of Joseph-Desire Mobutu. Mobutu later changed his name to Mobutu Sese Seko Kuku Ngbendu Wa Za Banga. Oddly enough, I was going to change my name to that until I found out that was Mobutu's full name.

Bastard! Mobutu not only murdered his political opponents, he kept his countrymen in utter poverty, and despair while paying himself handsomely. Mobutu resided in some amazing properties including a French Riviera Villa, a 15 acre beach resort, an enormous vineyard in Portugal, a huge mansion in Switzerland; and whose property portfolio is complete without a 16th century castle in Spain? It's sad the U.S. would choose to support a man so short sighted, greedy, and brutal. In the end the United States doesn't care how brutal a leader is. As President Franklin Delano Roosevelt said about Nicaraguan leader Anastasio Somoza "Somoza may be a son of a bitch, but he's our son of a bitch". Somoza was friendly to Wall Street, and in the end, what the U.S. fights for is our corporate greed.

Another well-known debacle that shows the United States immoral hypocrisy is the Iran-Contra scandal. They should make a movie about this. Oh wait, they did, a few actually, including "American Made" starring Tom Cruise, and "Kill the Messenger" starring Jeremy Renner. (Loved him in "The Town"). This is a well-known scandal where the Reagan Administration funneled millions of dollars to the brutal Contras through the illegal sale of weapons to Iran. The Contras murdered, raped, pillaged, and then with the CIA's help, trafficked cocaine. Gary Webb first reported the CIA's involvement, and knowledge of the Contra's shipping cocaine into the U.S. in his 1996 series for the San Jose Mercury News called the Dark Alliance. The Contras were flooding South-Central Los Angeles with cocaine, which was then turned into crack, helping create the crack epidemic of the 1980s. According to Contra leader Oscar Danilo Blandon the CIA felt the ends justified the means. Panamanian dictator Manual Noriega also helped bring arms to the Contras, and was allowed to traffic drugs using the same planes. Noriega, who was actually on the CIA's payroll as early as the 1960s, was often paid over $100,000 a year even though the CIA was well aware of General Noriega's drug trafficking.

It's strange to me how our government partakes in some of the most immoral acts one could think of, yet we still act as if we own the moral high ground compared to other countries. Gary Webb, who initially broke the story, was found dead of an apparent suicide. Mr. Webb shot himself twice in the head. I'm not saying the CIA helped him pull the trigger because there have been cases where individuals have shot themselves in the head twice while committing suicide, but it sure wouldn't surprise me if they did. It should be noted that 97% of all individuals who shot themselves in the head twice were either working with our government, mob informants, or had dirt on Hillary Clinton. (97% may be a slightly or almost completely made up percentage….. "may be").

I could go on nearly forever, and give case by case instances of corrupt acts that our government have been a part of that are the opposite of American ideals, but I don't think at this point that's a good use of the readers time. I just want you, the reader, to understand the depths of what our country gets involved with throughout the world, and how hypocritical it is of us to go wagging our finger at every other country like we are actually innocent. What I will do is list a few articles and their subject matter so you will get a pretty good idea on why the United States knows no end to its hypocrisy: In his March 8th, 2014 article for salon.com, Nicolas J.S. Davies titles and writes about "35 countries where the U.S. has supported fascists, drug lords and terrorists." Again, the leader can be a son of a bitch, as long as he's our son of a bitch. Another good read is an article in HuffPost by Ryan Grim and Arthur Delaney titled "The U.S. Has Been Meddling in Other Countries Elections for a Century. It Doesn't Feel Good." The information is out there, and it's endless, but for some reason we are not too bothered by our own immoral behavior.

Former CIA agent and writer Melissa Boyle Mahle stated in her 2008 documentary "Secrecy;" "Should we, as Americans be involved in kidnapping foreign people, and making them disappear?" "I would argue that's exactly the kind of thing we should be doing." I wasn't expecting Mrs. Mahle to say that, even if she was thinking it. That's the arrogant U.S. way of thinking whether it's the war on drugs or the war on terror. The United States somehow feels it's okay to kidnap citizens of other countries; and those kidnapped, especially when it's within the war on terror realm, often do not have many or any due process rights. 124 States are members of the International Criminal Court, but of course the United States is not. Noam Chomsky said it best in an interview by David Barsamian for the Monthly Review; Chomsky, in speaking about U.S. terrorist acts abroad, sums up my belief on why our international policies continue to create more anti U.S. terrorists. In referring to various U.S. acts that are terroristic, Chomsky states "They are known by the victims, of course, but the perpetrators
90

prefer to look elsewhere." It really is that brain washing that takes place in us all as we grow up and are taught our history. It's like Winston Churchill said "history is written by the winners". Are we just too lazy to go beyond what our government tells us? Do most of us just really not care enough if it's not happening in our own backyard? It's happening in countries most of us have no desire to visit. We go about our daily lives, and there is no room for the rage in us that we should have for what our government does around the world. Make no mistake about it, if you lived there, if that were your brother, your son, or your sister who was killed by a U.S. bomb or bullet you would find the room for the rage.

The U.S. government consistently lies to us citizens in order for us to get behind a war effort. It's been done multiple times throughout our history, and I think what the average person thinks is that was something that happened back then, not now. Of course that's not true, our government always has, and always will lie to us in order to lead us in the direction they want us to go. Everyone is familiar with the lies the Bush administration told us to invade Iraq but in the end, we accept that the administration lied and move on. In his August 26th 2002 speech, Dick Cheney stated "there is no doubt that Saddam Hussein now has weapons of mass destruction and is preparing to use them against our friends, against allies, and against us. Saddam also had biological and chemical weapons and has resumed his efforts to acquire nuclear weapons." On September 7th, 2002, then President Bush referred to an International Atomic Energy Agency report indication that

Saddam was "Six months away from developing a nuclear weapon." Too bad that fucker just made that garbage up. Apparently, the Bush/Cheney speechwriters thought their speeches should be factious.

I think all of us left-leaning individuals all expected and figured Bush and Cheney were lying, but when it came from Colin Powell I was thrown a little. Powell didn't come right out and support Bush's desire to invade Iraq, and seemed to be reviewing intelligence reports, and holding out on pressure from the White House to lie. In the end Powell gave in, and betrayed himself and his country when he told lies to the media, and in front of the United Nations. Lies, lies, and more lies. Yet, no one had any real consequences for their lies. Well, I mean no one who participated in spreading the lies. U.S. troops felt the consequences. Iraqi civilians certainly felt, and still feel the consequences. Of course it's always the poor in our country, and throughout the world who pay the price for the lies that lead us to war. From 2004 to 2009, more than 100,000 Iraqi civilians were killed. According to WikiLeaks reports, the vast majority of those civilian deaths were at the hands of fellow Iraqis but the deaths still stem from our illegal invasion. I think even that fact doesn't resonate at home like it should. Think about it; We, the United States of America, almost as pure of a country as a country can be, invaded another country. If any other country did this, we would be drawing up a U.N. resolution condemning the invasion, and probably eagerly preparing for our corporations to make millions of dollars selling weapons while we draw up plans to put our own troops in harm's way.

Our wars always leave behind unbelievable amounts of devastation for decades to come for both the countries we fight, and our own troops. The Vietnam War, and the secret bombing of Laos and Cambodia are great examples of how evil we can be as a country. The truth isn't really taught in American history books. Everything from making Christopher Columbus out to be some kind of hero, and a gentlemen, to our involvement in the overthrow of democratically elected leaders around the world. Lastly, to our government's lies, which get us into war, and how we conduct our wars.

I think the lies the Nixon administration told are well documented, and I don't see the need to rehash those. Even though the subject I will speak about is also well documented, I think we frame it in a way that makes its use not seem as inhumane. I'm talking about our use of chemical weapons during the Vietnam War. We often speak about other countries use of chemical weapons and how immoral those countries are, but I never hear about our use of chemical weapons. We were all taught about our use of chemical weapons, but in using the actual name of the chemical, it almost ignores the fact we used chemical weapons. This is especially true when a teacher is teaching the lesson to high school students. If a teacher is talking about the United States military's use of Agent Orange, I don't think most high school students make the connection; that using Agent Orange is using chemical weapons. Agent Orange is an herbicide. It was made to help clear forest cover, but I think we all can step back and know that our military didn't drop millions of gallons of a chemicals, and think it's only going to effect the foliage. An herbicide just sounds much nicer though, right? Agent Orange contains the deadly chemical Dioxin which doesn't sound quite as nice. From 1961 to 1971, the United States military, under program "Operation Ranch Hand," dropped over 20 million gallons over Vietnam, Laos, and Cambodia. It's sounding less nice by the minute isn't it? Although, I have to say "Operation Ranch Hand" sounds fairly kind. "Operation Ranch Hand" sounds like we might be helping farmers. Hmmm, Trump should have called his socialist program of bailing out farmers after his tariffs "Operation Ranch Hand" that would have been nice too!

The United States didn't stop with their use of Dioxin. The U.S. also continued its use of chemical weapons, and chemical warfare with their use of Napalm. Throughout the Vietnam War, the U.S. military dropped more than eight million tons of napalm incendiary bombs. Napalm burns between 1,500 and 22,000 degrees Fahrenheit. Think about that! Holy shit, where is our decency? How do you drop something like that on other human beings? It also blows my mind how those in power always talk about supporting our troops, but what they do is sacrifice our troops, not support them. The number we hear on how many American soldiers who died during the Vietnam War is 58,0000, with another 150,000 wounded. That number is horrible, but doesn't tell the true story of the herbicide, and the hell it unleashed. According to Nicole Fisher's May 28th 2018 article in Forbes magazine, an "estimated 2.8 million U.S. vets who were exposed to the poisonous chemical while serving and later died." It's so sad, and although many people don't care near as much, there were also more than 4 million Vietnamese citizens who were subjected to the Dioxin poison that was Agent Orange. Is that type of devastation the real legacy of the United States? I wish it were not, but at best it's a mixed bag of creating devastation in one regard, and being charitable in another. The charity we give is usually tied to some corporate profit, but that's not the subject here. Decades, and decades after we dropped millions of tons of bombs, Laotians are still being killed, and wounded by bombs that never exploded. To President Obama's credit, in 2016 Obama increased funding to help clear more unexploded bombs in Laos; but why on earth are people still getting killed almost 50 years after we dropped our last bombs in Laos? If you see the images of Laotians missing limbs, especially when it's children, you can't help but feel both sad, and ashamed at the same time.

The Vietnam War was really the first time American citizens completely understood our government couldn't be trusted. The U.S. government led its citizens astray with lies which led us to war. The anti-war movement was powerful, especially among young people who saw friends, and so many other young people go off to war, and die. Our government, and many right wing leaning individuals were disillusioned with the anti-war movement. The Kent State Massacre was a shameful response by our government, and a response that, as a brainwashed American, we wouldn't even think was possible here. On May 4th 1970, University students were protesting the bombing of Cambodia by the United States Military. Four unarmed, college students were shot, and killed by members of the Ohio National Guard. The four students killed were Jeffrey Miller, William

Schroeder, Sandra Scheuer, and Allison Krause. The following is a very brief history of the events that took place at Kent State followed by an interview with Laurel Krause, the sister of the 19 year old honor student, Allison Krause:

On May 2nd the National Guard arrived on the Kent state college campus. There were just under 100 National Guardsman and about 3,000 protestors. The protestors previously clashed with police and Kent mayor Leroy Satrom declared a state of emergency, and closed all local bars. The closing of the bars turned out to be a mistake as it actually led to more protestors showing up instead of being in a bar having a few drinks. Protestors set fire to the ROTC building and clashed with the firefighters who were trying to distinguish the fire. Due to the volatile nature of the protests on May 4th Ohio National Guard General Robert Canterbury ordered protestors to vacate the premises. Protestors refused to leave and began throwing rocks at various National Guardsman. The Guardsman were able to move protestors onto a football field, but also found themselves slightly trapped by the football fence and easy targets for some of the students who were throwing rocks. The National Guardsman eventually moved up a hill, called Blanket Hill, and this is where things went from bad to really bad. Somewhere between 25 and 30 of those National Guard members said to themselves, "shit, we have M-1 rifles, why are we retreating" upon this realization the guardsman began firing shots into the crowd killing four students, and injuring nine more. It was a sad day for America, and brought the anti-war movement to a whole new level. The following is a synopsis of my conversation with Laurel Krause.

On 10-04-2018 I had a brief, but interesting conversation with Laurel Krause, the sister of Allison Krause. You probably don't need the reminder since it was only about a page ago, but Allison Krause was the 19 year old honor student who was shot, and killed by the Ohio State National Guard during the Kent State student protests. Laurel is in her 60s now, but is still clearly effected by the death of her sister Allison. The pain in Laurel's voice was as if Allison had been killed 3 months, or perhaps 3 weeks ago. I have been lucky enough to never know what it's like to lose a sibling so I can only imagine the pain she felt, and is still feeling. Perhaps fighting for what Laurel believes is justice for Allison has been both a blessing and a curse for Laurel. I think fighting daily keeps the pain of losing a loved one right there on the surface. The pain can never be buried in the place where most of us bury ours. Part of Laurel's search for the truth was co-founding "The Kent State Truth Tribunal" with Emily Kunstler. Emily is an award-winning filmmaker and the daughter of civil rights attorney William Kunstler. Not one of the Ohio National Guardsman was every prosecuted. Originally, all eight were indicted, but the charges were later dismissed. That in itself had to be heartbreaking for the family members of those killed. We all want justice when we are wronged, and there is no worse personal feeling than feeling utterly powerless. I suppose that is the one thing all of us in the struggle fight for. We want some power over our own lives and in Laurel's case for those who can no longer fight for themselves. For those families of the four killed at Kent State, they received a lousy

97

$15,000 and a Statement of Regret. Evidence examiner Stuart Allen reviewed a tape of the Kent State Massacre and found an 'Order to Shoot'. This 'Order to Shoot' has been something Laurel Krause, and many others have suspected for many years. The Kent State Truth Tribunal is calling for the Attorney General to examine Mr. Allen's findings, and eventually receive an official acknowledgment for the Kent State shootings by the United States government. Laurel Krause also believes the FBI had an individual among the protesters who may have created the sound of a gun firing so the National Guardsman would have justification to return fire. Laurel spoke about COINTELPRO which she believes may have been involved.

According to encyclopedia Britannica COINTELPRO was an FBI counterintelligence program that ran from 1956 to 1971. The main goal of COINTELPRO was to "discredit and neutralize organizations considered subversive to U.S. political stability." The program often employed tactics that would be considered illegal. The program infiltrated groups such as the U.S. Communist Party, the Socialist Workers Party, the American Indian Movement, Ku Klux Klan, and spent much of their time on the Black Panther Party. It's even been rumored COINTELPRO sent Forest Gump to have a fight at a Black Panther Party. Some of the tactics COINTELPRO utilized were police harassment, surveillance, and anonymous mailings. The anonymous mailing tactic is something Laurel Krause believes was used to intimidate her family. Laurel and her family received a threatening letter that was supposedly from a neighbor, but Laurel and others strongly believe the FBI's COINTELPRO was behind the threatening letter. Laurel will continue her fight for justice for herself, her family, the families of those killed, and mostly for her sister Allison. If you would like to learn more about the Kent State Truth Tribunal you can go to www.truthtribunal.org

An extremely bothersome program that goes against everything America is supposed to stand for was the Bush/Cheney program of Extraordinary Rendition. The movie "Rendition" starring Jake Gyllenhaal and Reese Witherspoon is fantastic, and does a great job at showing the personal suffering that an individual goes through. I can find a great movie about every subject matter here that you should watch. I love movies. Okay, back to Extraordinary Rendition. The Extraordinary Rendition program didn't start under Bush/Cheney. The program was started in the early 1990s, but it was taken to a whole new level under Bush and Cheney. Extraordinary Rendition involves kidnapping or capturing individuals who are suspected of having some involvement in terrorist organizations. These captured individuals are then sent to countries such as Egypt, Syria, Jordan, Morocco, Saudi Arabia, Yemen, and Uzbekistan to face interrogations that involve torture. Former CIA agent Robert Baer classified the levels of torture used in various countries and in describing the use of torture in Egypt Baer stated "If you want someone to disappear – never to see them again – you send them to Egypt." Guess where the CIA sent most of their kidnapped souls? We've played this game before, and I think you know how it ends……..Egypt. Under the Bush/Cheney program it's estimated between 100 and 200 people were kidnapped and tortured, but who knows if we will ever learn the true number. Unfortunately I think most Americans don't care if we torture some suspected, Muslim terrorist. The United Nations General Assembly adopted the Convention Against Torture and Other Cruel, Inhuman or Degrading Treatment or Punishment in 1984. The Convention was approved and entered into force in 1987. The Convention defines torture as "any act by which severe pain or suffering, whether physical or mental, is intentionally inflicted on a person." The pain or suffering must be "inflicted by or at the instigation of or with the consent or acquiescence of a public official or another person acting in an official capacity." Article 3 of the Convention, which the U.S. clearly violated prohibits States from "expell[ing], return[ing] ('refouler') or extradit[ing] a person to another State where there are substantial grounds for believing that he would be in danger of being subjected to torture."

The United States signed the United Nations Convention Against Torture in October of 1994, but apparently the Bush administration thought they either found ways around violating our agreement or decided some forms of torture were not torture by their standards. Or I guess to the Bush administration, changing the name from torture to "enhanced interrogation techniques" was sufficient. Waterboarding is probably the most infamous torture technique that was used, but it certainly wasn't the only one. Let's take a look at some of these All American illegal uses of torture in these CIA enhanced interrogations. After you read each of these, take a few seconds and close your eyes and picture all these things happening to you.

Prisoners were often bound in stress positions. **Stress positions** include, but are not limited to having the person sit on the floor with your legs spread, and holding your hands straight up over your head, standing upright with your hands shackled to the ceiling, or having your feet shackled while holding your hands up. It's been reported that individuals would have to stand in their own feces, and urine. **Sleep Deprivation**, people were often kept awake100 hours straight. Sleep deprivation may not sound all that cruel, but as someone who has often went days without sleep, I can attest to how horrible it is, and my experience can't even compare to what they went through while being kept awake. **Cold Water Dousing,** where naked individuals who were shackled and handcuffed were doused in extremely cold water. A suspected Afghani militant held in a CIA black site named Gul Rahman died of hypothermia after being doused in cold water. I know, who cares, an Afghan militant, but the key word there is "suspected." **Cramped Confinement,** where people were confined to a box that would restrict their movement. The CIA agent/interrogator had the option do chose a box big enough to stand in where the agent could question the individual for up to 18 hours or 2 hours curled up tightly in a smaller box. **Facial Slaps, Beatings, and Threats,** beatings upon arrival, hard slaps to the face and back, and threats that their family would be harmed. Although I'm sure they did much more, I saved the best mental image for last for you, rectal feeding and rehydration. **Rectal Feeding and Rehydration**, where basically you puree food and insert it into their rectum. I'm not sure how that works, but I'm pretty sure you wouldn't get any nutrients by putting food in your ass, so please don't

101

try it. I mean, I'm not a doctor, nor do I play one on T.V., but I was in a couple awesome movies including Crimson: The Motion Picture. All by a film production company I'm a part of called White Lion Studios. (Sorry, I had to give us a plug). Whomever came up with rectal feeding, and rehydration was just a sick CIA pervert.

I hate terrorists. If I saw a terrorist burn someone to death, or cut off their head with a knife I would beat them to death with my own hands if I could. If I saw Dzhokhar Tsarnaev or Tamerian Tsarnaev after the Boston bombing, I would love to have killed them. The problem here is that many of these people were suspected terrorists who turned out not to be a terrorist, and their lives are wrecked. I know this happens in some CIA black site, or in Egypt, so it's out of sight out of mind. Who cares, but as I stated before if those tortured were your brother, husband, or your father, you certainly would care. All these suspected terrorists have sons, daughter, wives, cousins, and friends. After something like this happens, do they then love America or maybe more likely wish death to America? Torturing someone's family member or friend only deepens the resolve and heightens the animosity someone overseas may have about America. We have to be on that moral high ground we pretend to be on. Experts all agree torture does not produce reliable information. If a person is being tortured they will say anything to get you to stop. I think I'm hard as a coffin nail, but start torturing me, and I bet I will turn soft as cotton. They could kick me in the shins, and I will give the torturer some names. Of course the names I give them will be Judge Richard Arcara, and prosecutor Anthony Bruce. Trinity

College Dublin professor and author or "Why Torture Doesn't Work" Shane O'Mara argues "torture does not produce reliable information largely because of the severity with which it impairs the ability to think. Extreme pain, cold, sleep deprivation and fear of torture itself all damage memory, mood and cognition. Torture does not persuade people to make a reasoned decision to cooperate, but produces panic, dissociation, unconsciousness and long-term neurological damage. It also produces an intense desire to keep talking to prevent further torture." See, I told you.

Article 4 of The Torture Convention compels State Parties (meaning us) to criminalize acts of torture as well as "attempt[s] to commit torture" and "an act by any person which constitutes complicity or participation in torture." Complicity, that is the key word, and one I think about often with concern to the United States government. Our lawmakers are complicit in our prison industrial complex, our military industrial complex, as well as our act of aggression around the world. We know George Bush, and Dick Cheney are guilty here of war crimes for being complicit in torturing. We also know nothing will ever come from their guilt, and I like George Bush. I couldn't stand George Bush when he was President, but he has this childlike persona about him which makes me want to think he's not that bad of a guy, just maybe not that bright of a guy.

Donald Rumsfeld, George Tenet, Condoleezza Rice, John Aashcroft, Alberto Gonzales, as well as some high ranking military officers are all guilty of war crimes. Why? George Bush admitted he ordered waterboarding. Dick
103

Cheney still doesn't think there's anything wrong with waterboarding, and every one of those fuckers are complicit. Speaking of complicity; The U.S. didn't really like the use of the word "complicity" in the United Nations Torture Convention, so when the U.S. enacted their own legislation it was sort of bent to our will just in case we may need to find a way to torture someone. The U.S. senate adopted a reservation limiting the United States commitment under the United Nations Torture Convention. The United States Senate issued the following, "That with reference to Article 1, the United States understands that, in order to constitute torture, an act must be specifically intended to inflict severe physical or mental pain or suffering and that mental pain or suffering refers to prolonged mental harm caused by or resulting from: (1) the intentional infliction or threatened infliction of severe physical pain or suffering; (2) the administration or application, or threatened administration or application, of mind altering substances or other procedures calculated to disrupt profoundly the sense of the personality; (3) the threat of imminent death' or (4) the threat that another person will imminently be subject to death, severe physical pain or suffering, or the administration or application of mind altering substances or other procedures calculated to disrupt profoundly the senses or personality. (b) That the United States understands that the definition of torture in Article 1 is intended to apply only to acts directed against persons in the offender's custody or physical control.

This last sentence contained the key that unlocked the door for Attorney General Alberto Gonzales, Vice President

Dick Cheney and President George Bush. When Alberto Gonzales read "Article 1 is intended to apply only to acts directed against persons in the offender's custody or physical control" Mr. Gonzales instantly got erect, and said holy bleep!!! George, Dick, Dick, Dick!!! Why the hell did I "bleep?" I've been swearing all over the place, "Holy Fuck!!!" that's what Alberto said. Although if Mr. Gonzales would have read what the Foreign Affairs Reform and Restructuring Act of 1998 stated, maybe Mr. Gonzales would have changed his "Holy Fuck" reaction to "Awe fuck." I'm pretty sure he was quite aware of what the policy stated, but since you may not be, here it is. "It shall be the policy of the United States not to expel, extradite, or otherwise effect the involuntary return of any person to a country in which there are substantial grounds for believing the person would be in danger of being subjected to torture, regardless of whether the person is physically present in the United States." That's pretty clear Alberto.

As I stated previously the program of Rendition was started in the 1990's and although I'd love to place the whole shameful blame on the Bush Administration, the Clinton Administration did the exact same thing. The Republican Bush administration was worse, but the Democratic administrations of both Bill Clinton, and Barrack Obama shouldn't exactly be proud of their behavior in ignoring the United Nations Torture Convention. Under the Clinton administration, individuals were captured by the United States, sent to other countries under the Rendition program, and then executed by the country we sent them too. When Barrack Obama ran for President he often criticized the Bush administration for Extraordinary Rendition, but when Mr.

Obama became President Obama he suddenly didn't have the same moral fortitude as he did prior to becoming President.

Between continuing Rendition, and immensely increasing drone strikes; when it comes to those types of human rights issues, President Obama was not the change most informed, liberal minded people hoped for. Not that President Obama wasn't a huge improvement from the Bush administration. President Obama closed the CIA's secret black sites and no longer gave the CIA permission to use Bush and Cheney's enhanced interrogation techniques. As you can imagine, President Trump wouldn't have any moral qualms about rendition or torture. Actually, I can't imagine Trump would have any moral qualms about anything. I'm not positive, but I think in order to have a moral qualm, you would have to have morals. Nope, no morals or moral qualms for that man. Trump's pick for Director of the CIA was Gina Haspel. Mrs. Haspel operated former CIA black sites and drafted orders to destroy evidence that would have divulged torture. Trump continually talks tough, and threatens to bring back torture, but he has been highly secretive when it comes to what his administration is actually doing in the fight on terror.

Indefinite detention is horrible, and has shamefully remained in effect to this very day. Even if someone might be a terrorist, I don't see how anyone can think 15 years in prison without being charged or even allowed one day in some type of court could be okay. I get it, these people might be dangerous terrorists, but they might not be. I also understand that when many people hear their names, it
106

doesn't necessarily encourage empathy. The suspected terrorists names are Mohamed, Feras, or Ayman. If those who were locked up without even being charged were named Jacob, William, and James… maybe a little more outrage would be out there. To be fair, let's give credit where credit is due. First, the President on just his third day in office did order the detention facilities at Guantanamo to be closed no later than one year from the date of his order. President Obama wasn't able to get Guantanamo completely shut down, but President Obama did drastically reduce the prison population in Guantanamo. Currently there are only about 40 detainees remaining at Guantanamo, down from the more than 700 it contained at Guantanamo's height. Either way, 700, 400, or 40; just charge these people and if they are guilty, convict them and give them life in prison. As we all know, there are no shortages of prisons in 'Murica.'

Conclusion

There's just too much money involved so…..we're fucked, and so are the poor countries we continue to crush. Okay, you don't want to hear that bleak forecast. Unfortunately, when it comes to our military needs we have had the same mindset for 80 years now so we aren't going change that mindset in a few short years. We have to slowly decrease funding to the Pentagon. I don't think anyone can make the argument successfully that we need a military the size of ours to fight the current war on terror. I also don't see any way in which we can reduce our Military size quickly, and reintroduce tons of both skilled and unskilled individuals back into the workforce. I'm sure some people will be offended about the "unskilled" reference, but what I mean is those individuals may have skills that are relevant to life in the Marines, but not so much in the civilian world. We have to reevaluate how many bases are needed, and where those bases are needed. The bases can be slowly closed over a ten year period with plans to reeducate and re-skill those individuals reentering the civilian world.

I mentioned earlier we have approximately 35,000 troops in Germany and just under 40,000 in Japan. Do we need that many in those countries? No, of course not but maybe we can make everyone happy by keeping those bases open and keeping the troop count high or maybe even higher. Germany and Japan are countries we have great relationships with, and those countries do not see us as unwelcome guests. However, we offend many other countries by having bases in their back yard. When I was a kid, I got into a fight with a neighborhood kid who was in my backyard. If he wasn't in my backyard we probably wouldn't have gotten into a fight. Why the hell are we in everyone's back yard who doesn't even like us? We are uninvited house guests who show up with weapons, set up a spot in the corner of your backyard and never, ever, ever go back home.

Let's close Military bases in countries like Iraq, Afghanistan, and Qatar. By keeping many of our Military bases open in U.S. friendly countries, we will be able to keep our Military jobs program alive and well. We need to be smarter in how we deploy this jobs program. I would love to see our military get a complete overhaul but the reality is it's not going to happen, so let's try to come together on a solution that everyone can live with. I can accept that bases both home and abroad create jobs, and I'm okay with that, but we can also recognize that the military is a jobs program and make some adjustments to treat our military employees more like regular employees. For starters, how about we up the retirement age? To retire from the military, and receive a military pension, an individual must stay in the military for 20 years or more. Therefore if an individual retires as an E-8 after 20 years he or she will collect about $22,000 a year. Plus, if the retiree doesn't get their health benefits through a spouse, they can purchase a plan through Tricare at a much lower cost than traditional health insurance plans.

Most everyone is thankful to those who have served or are currently serving, but I think retirement age could be moved more along with that of the rest of our country which would save our country millions of dollars each year. Finally, an audit of the Pentagon's spending needs to (finally) take place. No one even has a clue as to the millions of dollars lost through waste and corruption. We have auditors who investigate certain aspects of waste of U.S. taxpayer funds but nothing as comprehensive as we need. Although, what these auditors do point out should make us angry enough, but as usual apathy is all we are capable of. Inspector general John Sopko pointed out billions of dollars in wasted funds in Afghanistan. The corruption included weapons disappearing as soon as they arrived, and planes being donated to local government that doesn't need them. Our corporations keep getting paid to produce the planes and weapons. The money is getting spread everywhere one way or another so our politicians are only too happy to pretend they are mad. Our politicians claim they are going to make changes but…... Sopko's report was done in 2012, and since then nothing has changed. The point is; if we stop the corruption, and if we spend our money wiser, we can keep an enormously large jobs program, cut down on the new terrorists we create, and spend the money we save on infrastructure and education.

Chapter-4

Democrats and Republicans
A One Party System?

-"Fascism should more appropriately be called corporatism because it is the merger of state, and corporate power." - Benito Mussolini-

As I began writing this book, I was dead set that we don't have a corrupt, two party system, but what we really have is a corrupt, one party system. With each passing day, and especially with Republicans being led by their current leader, I have to admit I've come to learn there are enough, serious differences between the two parties that I've changed my mind. Unfortunately, we are still left with a corrupt two party system, but one party is significantly better for 95% of us. It blows my mind how anyone who is not wealthy can be fooled by all these social issues into voting for the party that is laughing at you while they continue to be the real takers.

First off, let's make no mistake about it; Corporations, through their lobbyists, are running this country. I thought, incorrectly, that since big oil often not only does not pay taxes, but they actually have we, the U.S. taxpayers paying them in the form of subsidies; they would be the largest contributor to political campaigns. Energy industries rank number 9 in campaign contributions with the evil/influential

Koch Industries leading the way and contributing $5,698,840.00 through 2017-2018. Koch Industries contributions are not to be confused with the Koch brothers and their political networks donations. The Koch brothers laugh at nearly $6 million. With the Supreme Court clearing the way with their Citizens United decision, the Koch brothers and their like-minded friends spent $400 million in a losing effort to stop the reelection of President Obama. The network regrouped in 2013, and bought and paid for many Republican seats in the U.S. Senate, and they saved $100 million in the process. Go Cock brothers! I mean Koch, sorry. Like most corporations, those in the Energy field spend money on both parties, but the energy industry gives far more to Republicans. The top 5 are Republicans, all receiving about a half million or more with Democrat Heidi Heitkamp from North Dakota coming in at number 6 receiving almost a half million herself. However, 19 of the top 20 energy industry money grabbers are Republicans. The energy sector has over 600 firms and associations lobbying for their interests, so there is plenty of money to go around. However, when it comes to energy interests, especially oil corporations, their money is for the most part given heavily to Republicans.

So, what is the return on Oil and other energy companies lobbying investments? The return comes in various forms often in policies not being enacted. For example; Oil companies such as Exxon Mobile, Shell, and various others spend millions of dollars each year opposing climate change policies. The result of not having climate change policies enacted is fantastic for the oil companies, but horrific not just for the rest of the country, but for the rest of the world. Sometimes lobbyists have competing interests. The funny thing is when no one is lobbying for a bill it almost never passes. No money = No bill. I think that was one of Newton's Laws. Solar is at odds with the Utility companies; including electric, coal, and nuclear. Now, the Utility companies are fighting back, and slowing down the growth of solar power. Solar power in the U.S. has more than tripled since 2012 but the growth rate is slowing in large part because of push back, and push in of money from the Utility companies. Utility companies through lobbying efforts are getting some states to phase out "net metering," where a solar power owner can sell back power to the grid. Utility companies are also getting states to stop giving tax credits to individuals who purchase solar. Hopefully Governor Cuomo in New York never does either of these as solar is so important to our future and on a selfish note I just signed a contract to have solar panels installed on my home in Niagara Falls, NY.

California is truly leading the way when it comes to solar. California will require solar power for all new homes, and California law requires at least 50% of the state's electricity to come from non-carbon producing sources by 2030!!! Yayyyy California! I hope once other states see the success California has with solar they will follow their lead. California is committed to renewable sources of energy and is putting their money where their mouth is, but it's the non-renewable energy sources that unfortunately receive more subsidies. Clearly this isn't driven by what is best for our future. The subsidy amounts are driven by the dollars those industries can pour into campaign contributions and lobbying efforts. The U.S. fossil fuel industry is directly subsidized billions of dollars each year, and according to the International Monetary Fund (IMF) indirectly the oil industry costs tax payers trillions. Some of the costs are consumption subsidies, which are a good thing on the whole, but what if instead of subsidizing the consumption of fossil fuels we converted these low income homes to solar?

At least the solar panel companies will be paid off at some point. For example, I am getting solar panels installed to supply electricity to a 3400 sq. ft. home. I had to take out a 12 year loan, at 5% interest, which amounted to approximately $150.00 a month. The $150.00 dollar monthly payment amount is actually less than my current electric bill, and because my home has electric heat it will be about 4 times less in the winter months. Another indirect cost of the fossil fuel industry is the amount of time and money the U.S. military has to spend protecting shipping routes. Protecting oil and its shipping routes is another reason our Military needs such a significant presence in the Middle East. Lastly, the climate costs go far beyond the financial costs, and result in the loss of lives. According to Oil Change International, which is a research organization focused on showing the true costs of the fossil fuel industry; in the 2015-16 election cycle the energy industry, including oil, gas, and coal companies spent over 350 million dollars in campaign contributions, and lobbying efforts. In return for those investments or those contributions, and lobbying efforts they received almost 30 billion dollars in federal subsidies. As usual, campaign contributions, and lobbying efforts are money well spent.

Okay, you get the point on energy industries so let's focus a little on the number one lobbying industry. And the winner is…….The Pharmaceutical Industry! "Oh, thank you so much, we thought for sure the insurance industry, or oil and gas would win, but we are so proud of ourselves for never giving up and recognizing that spending 1 dollar in lobbying will earn us many, many more in sales. First, I'd like to thank the lobbyists. Without them we wouldn't be able to bribe congress with our contributions. Well, sure we could, but we'd have to do it ourselves. Second, and most importantly, we want to thank those we bribe (you know who you are) without you we might actually be in the free market system you pretend to love, and then we might have to sell our drugs for far less money, so thank you, thank you from the bottom of our bank accounts. Lastly, we do want to apologize quickly to those who started out on our pain killers, and who ended up on heroin. It was an unfortunate, unforeseen result that we never, ever, in a million years thought could be possible. Thanks again."

In 2018 the Pharmaceutical industry has spent over 150 million dollars in lobbying. The top spender was the Pharmaceutical Research & Manufacturers of America at almost $16 million with the number two contributor, Pfizer Inc. spending slightly over $6.5 million. The Pharmaceutical Research &Manufacturers of America is a trade group representing various companies in the pharmaceutical industry, advocating for public policies that make life easier and more profitable for those they represent. PhRMA represents companies such as 3M Pharmaceuticals, GE Healthcare, Johnson & Johnson, Merck & Co., Inc. and even the number two lobbying spender Pfizer Inc. Trump promised to use his amazing deal making skills to reduce the cost of prescription drugs but after meeting with top industry executives in Trump's first month in office, nothing has been done. Money talks and I'm sure those executives explained their role in contributing to the financial health of the Republican Party. Reportedly, the executives "educated" President Trump. I'm sure they did, they educated him on them being on the same money team as President Trump. The Pharmaceutical Research & Manufacturers of America not only lobby, but they advertise, and advocate for the pharmaceutical industry on the whole... and they have done a great job at shifting some of the blame away from the pharmaceutical companies.

While big Pharma is putting the blame elsewhere they are continuing to generate enormous amounts of money. In 2016, Johnson & Johnson generated revenue of 71.89 billion dollars while Merck & Co generated 39.49 billion. I feel like they should change the "&" symbol to an "$" symbol. Pfizer, (who are well known for their little blue pill), generated revenue of 52.82 billion in 2016 and like the effects of that little blue pill has on men, the future of Pharma revenue will continue to rise. Global Pharma is estimated to reach 1.12 trillion dollars in 2022. Roche is predicted to come in at number one with sales of 52.6 billion, Novartis comes in second with sales of 52.5 billion while Pfizer will round out the top three with sales just under 50 billion.

Both parties rake in the money from lobbyists and just like Hillary Clinton getting paid to give speeches to Wall Street, you're not giving out money without a pretty much guaranteed return on your investment. Four out of five of the 2018 top recipients from lobbyists are Democrats. The top five are; 1. Sherrod Brown (D-Ohio) $517,091.00 2. Jon

Tester (D-Montana) $497,213.00 3. Paul Ryan (R-Wisconsin) $453,131.00 4. Heidi Heitkamp (D-North Dakota) $444,666.00 5. Claire McCaskill (D-Missouri) $380,971.00

There's another sneaky way in which former Members of congress can use their connections and influence to earn themselves and their lobbying firms money. Former Speaker of the House Newt Gingrich, and former Senate Majority Leader Tom Daschle (who both sort of just fit that "sneaky" definition to a tee) work for lobbying firms, but never register as a lobbyist. Instead Gingrich and Daschle call themselves advisors, and are part of a revolving door between government and the corporate world. Gingrich denies being a lobbyist, and insists that his consulting firm "The Gingrich Group" solely provides strategic advice, not lobbying. I doubt there is any difference. Lobbying is by far the most popular and often lucrative career for a former member of Congress. The lobbying boom happened between 1998 and 2004 when almost half of all the 200 House members who left office for one reason or another became a lobbyist. Those leaving Congress at the end of more recent terms still often lobby, but like the aforementioned Newt and Tom, they often do it as "advisors" making a shady, corrupt system even more shady and corrupt.

The reason they call it a revolving door is that it's not just former Congressmen becoming lobbyists, but lobbyists who get jobs within the government in Washington. Does anyone actually believe they aren't working out deals with corporations they formerly lobbied for? It's like the saying goes, "when one door shuts, another opens" only this time it's everyone in Washington knowing

117

how the system works, and that they all must play the game, and they all get rewarded. The reward is money for campaigns, bills passed in congress, jobs for corporations you helped pass laws for, and jobs for lobbying firms. It's an endless cycle, and they are all getting filthy rich while we all pay the bill. Those "drain the swamp" policies Trump promised are lost here as well. Trump has almost 200 political appointees who were all former lobbyists. Geez, don't let the door hit you in the ass people.

As I stated earlier; both the Democrats and the Republicans are bought and paid for by corporations, but clearly how much corporations give to the two parties indicates who those parties look out for more, and where their values are (if they had any to begin with). I want to point out some significant differences between the two parties, and why all you middle class, and lower middle class Republican voters are about as stupid of a fool as a fool can be. Let's start with commercial banks like Wells Fargo, Bank of America, and JP Morgan Chase. In 2014, 72% of the industry's donations went to Republicans. The remaining 28% went directly to Hillary Clinton. (I'm kidding) Don't you know me at all by now? Looking at the 2017-18 range, the trend appears about the same. For example: of the $2,014,104.00 dollars the American Bankers Association donated, $1,502,903.00 dollars went to Republican candidates. JP Morgan Chase, Bank of America, and Wells Fargo all gave fairly equally to both parties with Republicans only getting slightly more. As you move to donations under a million dollars, the vast majority went to Republican candidates. Citizens First Bank and International Bank of Commerce gave 100% of their donations to

Republicans, while SunTrust Banks gave Republicans $361,671.00 of their $431,307.00 dollar total.

On the whole Democrats want some minor consumer protection bills that reign in the banks such as the Dodd-Frank banking reforms. The Republicans rolled back the Dodd-Frank with 33 of the 258 votes to pass it through the House coming from the Democrats. The bill eases restrictions on banks, and raises the threshold from 50 billion all the way up to 250 billion where banks are deemed too important to the financial system to fail. Now, those banks would no longer have to have stress tests that were put into place in order to avoid the exact financial disaster of why Dodd-Frank was enacted in the first place. You know who you think would be really upset about this? Former U.S. representative from Massachusetts Barney Frank. Do you know who isn't upset about the bill? You guessed it, Mr. Barney Frank. If he was still a member of Congress then I believe he would be enraged, but since Mr. Frank is a hypocrite who now works for the banking industry, good old Barney thinks this bill is fantastic, and now says the 50 billion dollar mark was far too low. The one thing I will say about Republicans, they are not hypocrites. They may fool the white trash dummies with social issues, but they make no bones about wanting all the money. Republicans never blamed the banks or thought the banks needed any regulation in the first place. Trump's 2019 budget proposal calls for 15.3 billion dollars in cuts to Medicare and 6.5 billion dollars in cuts in the first year alone to Medicaid. Republicans have wanted to privatize social security as well. You didn't make enough money in your lifetime to put enough aside to support yourself in retirement.....Fuck you.

119

You can't afford healthcare for yourself or your children…Fuck you. You didn't earn enough to pay for your own health insurance as a senior, or at least take on much more of the cost sharing……Well, Fuck you too, you old, poor bastard!

When it comes to climate change, Democrats seem to at least believe it's happening and understand it's actually a bigger threat to our security than the over-inflated threat of terrorism. Republicans either outright deny it or grudgingly admit to it, and usually add some kind of bullshit that's pro-business, and won't restrict polluting corporations in any way. Many Republicans also believe the good Lord will handle it, thus, this all must be a part of God's plan anyway. President Trump pulled the United States out of the Paris Accord in which 195 state parties have signed the agreement to strengthen the global response to the threat of climate change. In part, Trump pulled out because he got confused and thought he was supposed to do the same thing he did while having sex with Stormy Daniels. Trump is also motivated by his usual desire to undue everything President Obama did. Trump's administration is filled with climate change deniers and even if someone within the administration believes in the negative effects of climate change, I'm certain they understand they need to temper their voice for fear of Trump's wrath. Climate change deniers within Trump's administration include: Trump's Attorney General Jeff "the leprechaun" Sessions, Secretary of Energy, the guy who takes stupid to a whole new level, Rick Perry, Agriculture Secretary Sonny Perdue, Homeland Security Secretary Kristjen Nielsen, Vice President Mike

Pence, and the biggest idiot denier would be President Trump himself who thinks coal is the power source of the future. President Trump once stated "The concept of global warming was created by and for the Chinese in order to make U.S. manufacturing non-competitive."

Trump is constantly tweeting about it being cold outside as evidence that global warming is a hoax. Apparently Trump is confused, and doesn't understand the difference between climate change, and the weather. I could understand if he joked about it once or twice when it was super cold, but Trump has referred to global warming or climate change in over 100 tweets. Trump even removed climate change from the Pentagon's National Defense Strategy. Trump's ignorance on almost every subject knows no bounds, and you have to wonder does his cult now question the existence of global warming? Well, I just googled it and according to a 2017 article in the Washington Post only 25% percent of Trump supporters believed climate change is happening now and is caused by humans. I guess that's not exactly surprising. Trump supporters aren't exactly scientists are they? Although, you don't have to be a scientist to believe global warming exists, you just have to believe in science. I don't want to give Hillary Clinton supporters too much credit but 90% of Clinton voters at least believe global warming exists. Clinton voters still fall short of the 100% of Bernie believers who believed in both Bernie, and the fact that climate change is happening. (I made the 100% up, I'm fairly confident it's accurate, but I will allow for a 1% margin of error ☺).

Conclusion

Although corporate money is what dictates American policy at home, and around the globe there are significant policy differences between the two parties. If you are a multi-millionaire who has social views that line up with the Republican Party, then you should by all means be the asshole you are, and vote Republican. However if you are not wealthy, you have no business voting for Republicans. It goes beyond all levels of stupidity to vote against your own economic interests just because you're against gay marriage. What are the other reasons someone who is not wealthy is voting Republican? Welfare is often a subject that angers middle class Republican voters. I've heard Bernie Sanders make the argument that when a low wage Walmart or McDonald's worker is subsidized by collecting food stamps, we aren't actually subsidizing the worker, but we are subsidizing those companies, and their unwillingness to pay a high enough wage. If companies like Walmart paid a high enough wage then these workers wouldn't need government assistance. It's not as if Walmart can't afford to pay their employees a higher wage, they just refuse to so they can keep more of our money.

I have a brother who lives in Arizona who got hired for a skilled labor job, and they started him out at $12.00 dollars an hour. His kids are older so he doesn't have a family to support any more, but if he did the kids would either starve or they would need some help. My brother isn't someone who would take the help so I'm sure he would get a second job before he took any help, but why should he or anyone else have to, just so corporations can earn more of profit? I was putting a new roof on my house last summer, and afterwards I spoke to the gentleman who drove the truck, and loaded the bundles of shingles onto the conveyer belt for the rooftop delivery. I had given him a tip, and during our conversation the subject of wages came up. I asked him how much he made and he replied $13.00 dollars an hour. I was surprised that he had to drive a huge truck and load heavy bundles of shingles all for $13.00 dollars an hour. When I first heard the proposal of paying McDonald's workers $15.00 dollars an hour I thought it was too high, but as long as it's for full time workers it isn't too high. Plus, like the saying goes "a rising tide lifts all boats." The hope is if McDonald's or Walmart has to pay their full time employees a "livable wage" of $15.00 dollars an hour, how can these other corporations continue to pay low wages for skilled positions? The answer is they can't. These companies will have to pay these men and woman a respectable wage. It's not as if there isn't plenty of money to go around. Jeff Bezos, the owner of Amazon, makes more money in 10 seconds than the median Amazon worker makes in a year. I'm not saying the owner shouldn't make the lion's share of the money, but the greed of all these corporations is insane. We have to demand they spread the wealth around to more of their employees. Not to mention Amazon also paid no federal taxes in 2017! We have to tell our representatives this is unacceptable. Other social issues that get the majority of white voters who earn $30,000 to $50,000 dollars a year to vote Republican include immigration, racial tension, gay rights, the abortion issue, and lastly, another issue the Republicans do a fantastic job fooling the fools about is gun rights.

President Trump himself claimed if Democrats win a majority in Congress "they'll take away your 2nd Amendment." The false claim that Democrats want to take away your guns is a belief firmly held by most uneducated, lower income Republican voters. Republicans spread the lies, and fuel the fire, but as usual there's no truth to what they are saying. Democrats are gun owners who often have the same limited understanding of the Second Amendments original intent as the unintelligent Trump voter does. The Second Amendment was ratified in 1791 and states "A well regulated Militia, being necessary to the security of a free State, the right of the people to keep and bear Arms, shall not be infringed." I don't know anyone in a fucking Militia. Do you? Without spending much more time on this; The second amendment was written when you could actually rise up against your tyrannical government, and attempt to overthrow it. Go ahead, get 20,000 of your best buds together, and give it a shot. See how fast our government crushes you. Democrats want some sensible gun laws that almost everyone is in favor of. The Democrats do not want to take your guns, or give theirs up either for that matter. We need to kick the Republicans out of office and keep them out. Then once they are out we need to start kicking the Democrats out next. This narrative that 3rd Party candidates can't win has to be changed, or we have to change the Democratic Party, and I don't mean just moving it to the left on the social   issues. Corporations have to stop controlling

124

our country. They are the reason we drop bombs everywhere. They are the reason we have a CIA that does things around the world that make other countries wish we were like Russia and only created bullshit memes. They are the reason we spend more money on healthcare than any other country yet we don't see better health outcomes. This is supposed to be a government of the people, for the people, and by the people. However, what we have is a government of the corporations, for the corporations and by the corporations. We need to kick all these greedy corporations the hell out of our government! I think first, we may have to kick the politicians out though...

Chapter-5

African Americans in America

On my first day of kindergarten I met Tony Blackman, and that day or sometime that week he came over my house to play. I also met Willie Santiago who I also brought over my house that week. My dad, who up till the day he died was a workaholic, happened to stop home briefly both days, and met both Tony and Willie. My father could have said, "You can't bring home black and Puerto Rican kids to play with," but he didn't. The only thing I remember my father saying was "they seemed like nice kids." I also remember going to my grandma and grandpa Bellavia's house on Sundays at 1:00 p.m. for macaroni and meatballs. My grandfather being from a different era and generation was very racist. I remember watching basketball or football games, and that's all I would hear out of his mouth was "nigger this," and "nigger that" and I hated it. I couldn't stand going there, and listening to him. When we were on his porch my grandfather would point out houses in the neighborhood where he and my grandmother lived in downtown Niagara Falls, NY, and say "that used to be Italian or Polish, and now a nigger lives there," and etc. etc. Magic Johnson was one of my heroes growing up so when I saw Magic running and smiling, I saw someone I wanted to be, not what my grandfather saw. I emulated Magic Johnson, Byron Scott, and James Worthy of the Los Angeles Lakers; not Larry Bird, Kevin McHale or Danny Ainge of the

126

Boston Celtics. When I played football I was Lynn Swan, James Stallworth or Terry Bradshaw of my favorite NFL team the Pittsburgh Steelers. Okay, Terry is white, but what the heck, I'm not racist against white people either so leave me alone.

I'm so glad that I didn't hear racist language in my own house growing up. In more current times my ex-girlfriend CeCi Colvin and her son, Aaron Shareef are black and my family loved them as much as they love me. (They may like them even more) I'm so glad I wasn't taught to be a racist at home, even if my grandfather tried once a week. Racism is learned at various points in our lives. I think we all have a little racism in us, even if it's just thinking our ethnicity is the best. I'm Italian, and there isn't anything else I'd rather be. I love the food, I love my big Italian family, and everything that comes along with being Italian. There's no other ethnicity I'd rather be so that automatically makes me slightly racist against all other ethnicities I think. That's as far as it goes for me though. I love all people, and I feel that everybody has amazing cultural gifts to offer. My best friend is an Arab and I love his family. They are very similar to my own. They are kind, all close with one another, and are always offering you something to eat or drink when you go to their house. Very much like Italians. When I went to prison, and received a sentence that was based on conduct I was found not guilty of, I felt I was denied a constitutional right I was born with. I can only imagine that's how many African Americans often feel. The most famous words in the Declaration of Independence are "We hold these truths to be self-evident, that all men are created equal; that they are endowed by their Creator with certain unalienable Rights, that among these are Life, Liberty, and the pursuit of Happiness." Last night I went to see The BlacKkKlansman with my good friend Michael Esposito. The movie wasn't great, and started out slow, but the last 30 minutes were very good, and the last two minutes or so were powerful, and almost brought a tear to my eye.

Here we are 242 years after slave owner Thomas Jefferson wrote those famous words in the Declaration of Independence, and I'm watching a clip of racist, white nationalists marching in a 'Unite the Right' rally in Charlottesville. I watched the rage-filled James Alex Fields drive his car into a crowd killing Heather Heyer. They also showed clips of Donald Trump shamefully talking about the march, and referring to the Neo Nazis as "good people". The ending was sad, and everyone in the theater walked out in silence. It's so sad that all these years later, and some groups in America still do not have the same right to "Life, Liberty, and the pursuit of Happiness" because clearly many Americans do not believe all men are created equal. Maybe that was inevitable when even after the death of the declarations author, 130 of those enslaved at Jefferson's Monticello plantation were sold from an auction block. We certainly have come far, but holy shit, not near far enough.

An issue I couldn't wait to address is the NFL's kneeling controversy. To me, this is such an important topic, and all you have to do is scroll down your Facebook wall for 30 seconds to see how it is on so many of your ignorant friend's minds. I'm constantly seeing different memes or statements on how, if they see these spoiled, rich athletes taking a knee they won't watch the NFL again, etc. etc. etc., (well unless their team is winning, then they will watch).

First off, let me say, if I were African American, I'm not so sure I would ever stand for the National Anthem for a country which has never afforded me equal protection under the law. In the end that's what all this boils to; equal protection under the law. First off, the National Anthem itself was written by a racist, and has an extremely racist third verse which was removed. The third verse of the Star-Spangled Banner goes as follows "and where is the band who so vauntingly swore, that havoc of war and the battle's confusion a home and a country should leave us no more? Their blood has wash'd out their foul footstep's pollution. No Refuge could save the hireling and slave, from the terror of flight or the gloom of the grave, and the star-spangled banner in triumph doth wave, o'er the land of the free and the home of the brave." Author Frances Key Scott was a DC prosecutor who believed anyone who possessed abolitionist literature should receive the death penalty. That's a bit hard Frances. So, this is the song that you expect African Americans should stand at attention for? Most people aren't even aware of that racist verse. The full version or the history behind the full version of the Star-Spangled Banner certainly isn't taught to us in school.

Now let's briefly run through the history of African Americans in the United States, and see if we can find a time where they have enjoyed this all important concept of equal protection under the law. This won't even be close to a full history, and will leave many important people and events out. This book isn't written for historians, it's written to give the average person a nice overview so they can see where America has been, to say the least, imperfect. This is somewhat debatable as to whether or not the 19 Africans

brought to Jamestown, Virginia in 1619 by Dutch traders were slaves or indentured servants, but I think as far as painting a picture of African Americans journey in the U.S. we can start here. So from the early 1600's to the passing of the Thirteenth Amendment in December of 1865 African Americans were slaves. Technically with Abraham Lincoln's Emancipation Proclamation in 1863, slavery was effectively ended, but again for painting the picture we don't need to get caught up in every detail. After slavery ended, we have the failed Reconstruction era, which ended with the Compromise of 1877. When I write "failed" that's not to say the Reconstruction era was a complete failure with no successes, but it ended far too soon and with far too many promises unfulfilled. If the 'Forty acres and a mule' promise was fulfilled, newly freed slaves would have had land, and wealth to pass down to their children. Instead, almost all land allocated during the war was restored to its pre-war owners. The whole plight of African Americans could have been different. Black Codes were brought about in late 1865 in Mississippi and South Carolina. Mississippi kept newly freed slaves down by requiring black individuals to have written evidence of employment for the coming year every January. If these newly "free" people left before that year contract was completed they would have to forfeit wages already earned or be arrested. South Carolina also had Black Codes in the form of laws which forbade black people from having any job other than being a farmer or a servant. If somehow any newly freed black person did get a job outside of these two areas they were forced to pay an annual tax of anywhere from $10.00 to $100.00 dollars. Black people were often charged with vagrancy and made to work right back
130

on a plantation. So much for freedom.

After the Reconstruction Era, African Americans, as you could imagine, still had a difficult time finding work; thus many African Americans remained sharecroppers or tenant farmers. Basically, they were back to where they started with being indentured servants or perhaps slaves minus the slave drivers. Segregation continued with Jim Crow laws, and the Supreme Court's 1896 ruling in Plessy v. Ferguson of "separate but equal." Throughout this time as African Americans struggled to find any economic stability, and dealt with separate but equal, they also had to contend with the severe violence of the KKK. Founded in 1866, the KKK was everywhere in the South by the 1870s, and it wasn't like those who fled to the Northern States were living fantastic, prejudice-free lives while receiving amazing educations so they could prosper and be accepted as equals. The height of both the KKK's membership and violence was in the 1920's with lynching's, beatings, and burning crosses commonplace. African Americans lived in both fear, and poverty.

WWII brought some hope and relief to African Americans simply because there was a demand for labor, and military service. Hope for those who served came in the thought that if they served their country, then their country would accept them as equals upon their return..... not exactly, sorry. Voter suppression continued with only 2% of Southern African Americans being registered to vote, but that slowly began to rise and hit about 12% in 1947. Still, 12% is not exactly having your voice heard, and voting itself was always met with both violence, and laws to make it nearly impossible. Then we have the civil rights era from

1954 to 1968 with the culmination being the passing of the July 2nd 1964 Civil Rights Act by then President Lyndon Johnson. There were many notable achievements and milestones during the civil rights era. The civil rights era saw Rosa Parks thrust into the movement, and with the help of many including Martin Luther King Jr., organized the boycott of the Montgomery bus system. Due to continued voter suppression, President Dwight Eisenhower signed the Civil Rights Act of 1957, allowing federal prosecution of anyone who tried to prevent someone from voting. In August of 1963, over 200,000 people marched on Washington, D.C. with Martin Luther King Jr. making his famous "I have a dream" speech. This August of 1963 march is the exact thing that is needed to change our current "lock every African American up in prison" policies. Again, another voting rights act was needed because voter suppression was still running rampant in the south. President Johnson signed the Voting Rights Act of 1965 which banned all voter literacy tests, and provided federal examiners in various jurisdictions. Finally, the Fair Housing Act of 1968 made it illegal to discriminate in housing based on race, sex, national origin or religion. As I wrote about earlier, housing discrimination was still something African Americans had to deal with and segregation was always at the heart of the matter because many white Americans did not want African Americans living in the same neighborhoods as they resided.

Now we are moving into the 1970's which isn't exactly ancient history. Although federally funded segregated housing began with Roosevelt and the New Deal, the 1970's saw an explosion of Section 8 project-based housing. Segregation is always something our government has been keen on, and really still is to this very day. Integration was fought even in the North with some of the most violent protests about school integration taking place in Boston. Underfunded schools with no resources were a constant theme for generations of African Americans. African Americans made many strides politically, socially, and economically throughout the 1970's and 1980's. In 1971, there were only 8 African American mayors, but by the mid-1970's there were 135 total. Unfortunately, the 1970's began a new form of segregation which continues today. Our government's new form of segregation is moving African Americans from their inner city housing units to prisons.

The 1980's also saw the crack epidemic which was spurred along by Reagan and the CIA's involvement with the Contras. Prior to the mid-1980's the average prison sentence for African Americans was six percent higher than whites, but by 1990 the average sentence for African Americans was over 90% higher than whites. This was due in large part to the sentencing differences for powdered cocaine compared to crack cocaine. Segregation continued to be the theme for African Americans in America, and the 1990's were no different. In New York State, 80% of African American children attended predominately underfunded black schools. Lack of education leads to lack of opportunities, and lack of success.

Bill Clinton's Presidency saw the implementation of draconian drug laws including the three strikes you're out crime bill. President Clinton put 100,000 more police officers on the streets and admittedly "locked up minor actors for way too long." It's easy for a politician like Bill Clinton to admit their mistake after the fact, but I don't in any way think these decisions weren't made not knowing exactly what was going to be the result. His policies helped create more jobs for one segment of the population while locking up another. Incarceration numbers in recent years have gone down slowly with the States leading the way. President Obama did far too little with the only reforms being passed during his administration being the 2010 Fair Sentencing Act, which reduced crack-cocaine penalties, and the Second Chance Pell Pilot Program, which allowed incarcerated Americans to receive Pell Grants to pursue post-secondary education programs.

Under President Trump, racism has moved more out in the open again, but hopefully when Mr. Trump is impeached that will slowly end. Trump understands he can lead the rhetoric that many racists love, whether it's about NFL players kneeling or police brutality. I'm not saying the police are always wrong, but certainly the prospect of being shot and killed even while doing what you're instructed to do is real for many African Americans; especially African American males. For easy viewing, I'm going to put a brief bullet point history of why if African American athletes feel they need to respectfully take a knee to shed light on social injustices, you should shut the fuck up and try having some empathy.

Brief timeline-

-1619 to 1865, Slavery
-1865 to 1877, Failed Reconstruction
-1877 to 1950's, Jim Crow, Separate but Equal and
    massive KKK led violence
-1954 to 1968 The Civil Rights Era saw progress, poverty,
    and more violence
-1970 to Present, Continued segregation through leased
    housing, and the start of mass incarceration which
    continues to this very day
-Lock them up, lock them up, lock them up

If you are white, can you imagine going through all
that violence, and discrimination simply because the color of
your skin is darker than the color of someone else's skin? It's
so simple; solely because their skin color is darker, they have
endured murder, rape, slavery, segregation, and fear.
African Americans along with many of their white brothers
and sisters (kind of stealing that from one of my heroes
Cornell West) fought tooth-and-nail for every right they
have today. Again, if you're white can you imagine having
to fight for every right that others were just born with? Can
you imagine being somewhere, and wondering if someone
dislikes you for no other reason than the color of your skin?
Can you imagine being pulled over on a dark night, and
having the thought of wanting to make sure you do
everything right because you know the situation could
escalate, and you could end up in jail or dead? Can you
imagine never once having equal protection under the law?
Can you imagine not being able to respectfully take a knee
135

in silent protest with tons of people flipping out, and acting as if you have no reason or right to respectfully protest just because you're an athlete who makes a lot of money? First off, that is the exact reason they should be taking a knee. NFL or NBA players have the forum to bring attention to an issue that's important to them. If they were Joe the bus driver taking a knee would anyone care? No, of course fucking not. I wasn't a big Kaepernick fan as a QB, but certainly he's good enough to at least be the backup for almost all NFL teams. The reason Kaepernick isn't playing in the NFL is because he's clearly being black balled. Anyway, if you don't understand why NFL players should be able to take a knee you're either ignorant or racist. Which one are you?

Racism has certainly changed. Prospects for achievements by African Americans are better than ever. If you are growing up as a black male or maybe even some females may disagree with that statement, but go talk to your grandparents or any elder in your family, and I'm sure they will agree with me for the most part. Today's racist looks different than the one of years past. Today's racist looks like some of my old friends on Facebook, who aren't really my friends anymore. Today's racist looks like some of my family members. Today's racist, in my opinion isn't as bold faced, violent, or dangerous as in years past. Although, like I wrote earlier, Trump has reinvigorated, and embolden racist behavior to be more out in the open again. However, in general, today's racist will be kind to your face, and talk shit behind your back. Today's racist will hire you to work for them. Today's racist can judge you as an individual.

Nevertheless, today's racist has a poor opinion of the African American race on the whole, with no understanding of how history directly ties into their present struggles.

If throughout the history of a certain group of people, that group was continually denied access to opportunities and resources, how would you expect that group to have the same level of success as another group? Kids born from educated, wealthy parents are going to grow up, and become educated, wealthy adults. The process continues generation after generation because they are afforded completely different opportunities then a kid who was born into a family that is poor, and uneducated. Being born to poor, uneducated parents doesn't mean you can't achieve, but it certainly makes it more difficult. Then throw centuries of discrimination into the mix and see where you end up. I always say if life is a marathon then if you're a black male you're often starting out 50 yards behind the end of the pack. There is nothing genetically inferior about an African American, a Latino American, or any other race when comparing them to another. Part of the problem with today's racist is he doesn't see oppression like he once saw in the history books. I try to explain to people that time doesn't exist in a bubble. When talking about the difficulties faced today, you have to tie it into yesterday, and the yesterday before that, and so on till you get to the beginning. Then you should be able to draw the line between today, and yesterday, and see that it's all interconnected, and maybe instead of feeling anger when you see someone taking a knee, you will have empathy and compassion.

The Black Lives Matter movement started out on

shaky ground for me. The Black Lives Matter movement started out as the hashtag #BlackLivesMatter after George Zimmerman's acquittal of killing Trayvon Martin. It's not that under normal circumstances I didn't think George Zimmerman shouldn't have been convicted, but the stupid ass State of Florida has a stupid ass "stand your ground" law. The Stand Your Ground law needs to be done away with, it's ridiculous, and has no place in our world. If you are defending yourself then you can use a "Self Defense" defense. Stand Your Ground takes that defense to another level, as well as taking stupidity to another level. The real problem in this case isn't that George Zimmerman was acquitted under Florida's current law, but that Mr. Zimmerman was racially motivated to protect his community from what he perceived as a threat based simply on the fact that Trayvon Martin was black. If Trayvon was white, Mr. Zimmerman probably still would have watched him initially, but then Mr. Zimmerman would have figured the person was walking home or to a friend's house, and let him be. However, because Trayvon Martin was black Mr. Zimmerman assumed the worst, and because Mr. Zimmerman assumed the worst, Trayvon Martin ended up dead.

The Black Lives Matter movement is something I understand the need for, and support, but it's also something that needs some changes. The need for those changes makes me less vocal in my support. There are times like when Charleston, South Carolina Police Officer, Michael T. Slager shot/murdered a fleeing Walter L. Scott where Black Lives Matter needs to be there protesting. When something like that happens, I always think, "can you imagine how many times something like that was done, and not filmed, and the cop lied about it?" If that wasn't caught on cell phone video, that Police Officer would have lied, and said Mr. Scott attacked him, and tried to get his gun, or he would have planted a gun on him, and he would have gotten away with murder. Throughout the years that's happened thousands of times, and when it happens, Police need to be held accountable, just as any citizen would. Furthermore, other Police Officers need to call that person out instead of defending their actions. I see horrible conduct consistently defended by officers when a fellow officer gets caught doing something wrong. Many times CNN or some other news organization will interview some retired captain or an officer, and instead of calling out their fellow officer, he or she defends them. It's disgusting, and does them no good.

On the other hand, I don't think it was clear that, in the Ferguson shooting of Michael Brown, the Police Officer was in the wrong. Maybe he was, but from everything I've read it seems Officer Darren Wilson may have been justified in shooting Mr. Brown. There are problems on both sides in this instance though. Perhaps Black Lives Matter should have some sort of waiting period to let some facts come out before protests begin. I think when protests begin right away then details come out where the individual is on drugs, and or attacked the officer then it puts in question the movement's credibility in many people's eyes. On the other hand the U.S. Department of Justice released a report that showed racial discrimination at disturbing levels so it's a wonder why the mistrust of Police was at a level where waiting wasn't even part of their thought process. Federal officials learned that city officials worked together with law enforcement to generate as much money as possible from fines and court fees. This often helps keep lower income people poor and desperate, and then if they can't pay their fines they end up in jail. Hmmm, I kind of remember reading a similar tactic that was done in 1865 in Mississippi, and South Carolina. Do you remember reading it? I hope so, it was only a couple pages ago. In Ferguson, the city relied on the police department and the courts to generate revenue to fill budget gaps. Racial profiling seemed to be rampant in the Ferguson Police Department where from 2012 to 2014, 85% of individuals who were pulled over were African American. The most telling issue that shows severe prejudice is when African Americans were pulled over they were almost 2 ½ times more likely to be searched, leading to 93% of those arrested being black even though white individuals were more likely to have contraband. Personally, I don't think anyone should be able to be searched when pulled over. It's more bullshit about how we are the freest country in the world, yet I can't go two blocks without seeing a police vehicle. I'm not sure how it is with State Troopers in other states but in New York they seem to exist solely to write tickets to pay their own salaries. State troopers not only write tickets on the NY State thruway, but they come into the poor cities of Niagara Falls and Buffalo and write tickets, which is completely ridiculous. State troopers coming into poor cities truly hurts the local population's ability to spend money at local restaurants, and contribute to the local economy in general. It's not as if State Troopers come in and help local police by responding to a domestic call or something more pressing. No, State

Troopers exist solely to generate money for themselves and the State.

If a police officer murders someone, the officer needs to be charged, and then convicted just like the rest of us would be. Part of the problem is that everyone in the justice system are all on the same team. You don't see members of the same football team tackling their own running back, well, unless they play for the Cleveland Browns, then they might. First off, it's almost impossible for an officer to get indicted, so if they do, you can bet the prosecutor must have had no choice in the matter. More than likely if an officer was indicted it was caught on film, and therefore it was followed by public outcry. Then, the prosecutor and their team got together to see if there was any way possible they could not indict the officer. This attempt not to charge the officer is the complete opposite of what they do when it's a public citizen. Nearly every year police officers kill approximately 1,000 people. That's a lot of dead people. I'm sure the officers in many or most cases are in the right or had no choice, but I'm also sure that in many instances they did not have to kill the person.

Let's take the murder of 40 year old Terence Crutcher. Tulsa Oklahoma police officer Betty Shelby murdered Mr. Crutcher, and I don't care what anyone else says because they are full of shit. I watched the YouTube video many times, and there is no way in hell that Betty Shelby needed to kill Mr. Crutcher. Officer Shelby had another officer right beside her, and there were at least four officers on the scene because two more were right behind her. Not to mention it was 45 minutes before someone finally approached Terence Crutcher's body to administer any type of CPR, and
141

although I'm not a doctor, I'm pretty sure it was a little too late for that. Umm, thanks for trying though??? Do you know when it's a pretty good indication the officer was completely wrong for killing a black guy? If you guessed when Donald Trump comes out and says so, you would be correct. Mr. Trump stated that the video had him feeling "very, very troubled." Mr. Trump went on to state "That man went to the car, hands up, put his hand on the car. I mean, to me, it looked like he did everything he's supposed to do." Come on, even Donald Trump is saying you, a black guy, did everything right, and his family still can't get justice. So what happened when Officer Shelby went to trial? The same thing that happens many times when officers go to trial, Officer Shelby was acquitted. That's complete bullshit, and if Betty Shelby wasn't a cop she would be in prison right now, plain, and simple.

The number of people killed by police officers is pretty consistently close to 1,000 a year, and between 2005 and 2017, 80 officers had been arrested for either murder or manslaughter. The bar is set pretty high for an officer to be charged in the first place so I would assume that of those 80 officers at least 90% were convicted. Well, you know what they say about how you should never assume. I guess they made an ass out of me because only about 35% of those 80 police officers were convicted. Most, like Officer Shelby, were acquitted and then went back to work on the force. If you're a regular citizen in the real world and you go to trial, the conviction rate jumps up to 92%. As my awesome Uncle Sal always says "Un-fucking believable." Actually, I've never even heard my Uncle Sal swear before, but he is awesome.

Black Lives Matter is needed because we all recognize the fact that All Lives Matter, but it's painfully obvious America has not completely realized that "black lives" are included in "all lives." I'm pretty sure no other group of people would love it more than black people if there were no need to have a Black Lives Matter movement. The movement isn't perfect. As I stated, I would like to see a waiting period before protests begin. If a Police Officer is clearly in the right then I would like to see Black Lives Matter come out with a statement in support of the police. Black Lives Matter has a network now with over 40 chapters so I'm sure it's difficult to organize, but I'd like to see Black Lives Matter come together and address various other problems within the black community, and not just to protest during the times of police brutality.

The debate on black-on-black crime seems to be a contentious issue on both sides. I've heard racist people speak about it with no acknowledgement of the issues that cause it. I've also heard African Americans speak about it, and basically deny it's an issue or say it's racist to even bring it up, which is both counterproductive, and ridiculous. Before I get into the subject, I want to be clear in my thought that black-on-black crime is a completely separate issue from an officer of the law killing an unarmed African American, or a White American for that matter. Police are killing far too many people in general. In 2016, police officers shot and killed 50 unarmed black people, and they also shot and killed 50 unarmed white people. It's actually true that more white people are shot and killed by the police every year, but when you take population numbers into consideration,
143

African Americans are 2 ½ times more likely to be killed by the police than white Americans. Police officers are agents of the state who are paid to protect and serve so you shouldn't have to ever worry about being shot for little or no reason at all. Anyway, those are two separate issues, and I don't think it's fair if we are talking about the number of unarmed black people shot by police to say, "yeah but more black people died by other black people killing them." So, that makes it okay? No, of course it doesn't, and that's one of the reasons they are separate issues, and have no business being lumped together.

Black-on-black crime is real though, just as white-on-white crime is real. The recurring theme of segregation and poverty are the main causes, but there are also other issues that need to be addressed. The reasons white people commit crimes against other white people is they tend to live in white neighborhoods. The same reasons apply to black people who commit crimes against other black people, because they often live in neighborhoods that are primarily black. The issue of black on black or white on white crime isn't exactly rocket science as to how it happens that way, but it's also not so simple that we can just end the conversation right there either. It is as simple as proximity as far as why it's white-on-white or black-on-black crime, but the amount of crimes or why those crimes are committed are different.

I read an article from October, 2017 in The Root by Michael Harriot titled "Why We Never Talk About Black-on-Black Crime: An Answer to White America's Most Pressing Question." I was a little surprised because in my opinion Mr.

Harriot came off as very racist in the article. In the last two years, I unfriended 5 white people for racist comments, and 4 black people for their racist comments. I write this because I will not put up with racism no matter who or where it comes from. Even the title itself was offensive, "An Answer to White America's Most Pressing Question." First off, it's not white America's most pressing question by any stretch of the imagination, and for most of us if we are speaking about that subject it's because we care. Unless you're a Fox News watching, Trump supporting racist, the question of black-on-black crime is asked to find out what can be done to solve it, not to place blame. An early point I reject from Mr. Harriot's article is "It's not a thing." The reason Mr. Harriot uses as to why it's not a thing is because white-on-white crime exists. Well, just because one thing exists, it doesn't mean the other does not exist. The two issues don't cancel each other out. It just means they both exist. Shootings kill more than 36,000 Americans every year. That means close to 100 people every single day are killed by being shot. An even more startling figure is between 2001 and 2014; 440,095 people were killed by firearms in the United States.

Mass shootings are defined differently by different organizations, thus their statistics vary greatly. The non-profit organization Gun Violence Archive defines mass shootings by four or more individuals either killed or wounded by a shooter in one incident. The liberal magazine Mother Jones defines mass shootings as "a single attack in a public place in which three or more victims were killed." In 2017, there were 273 shootings that met the criteria set by Gun Violence Archive. The data on who commits the

145

majority of mass shootings ranges depending on the study with a study done by Mother Jones putting the percentage at 54% committed by whites while Grant Duwe, author of "Mass Murder in the United States: A History" puts it at 63%. Mr. Duwe does go all the way back to 1900, while Mother Jones's study went back to 1982. It's actually insane that something in our control is killing close to 100 people a day, and yet we do nothing about it. Gun violence is a huge problem concerning white-on-white crime, and black-on-black crime. Concerning gun related deaths, White Americans are more often involved in mass shootings, shootings of their spouse, and suicided. African Americans deaths relating to gun violence are vastly different than was described concerning white gun violence. According to the Centers for Disease Control and Prevention, African Americans are eight times more likely to be shot and killed by guns than white Americans are. Even though African Americans are only about 13% of the population, black individuals are killed more by guns in all 50 states; African Americans account for 51% of all homicide victims in America. Mr. Harriot's second point of "It has nothing to do with what we are talking about," only makes sense if you are trying to talk about police violence, and someone dismisses that just because there is black on black crime. As I stated, they are two separate issues. Mr. Harriot writes "Imagine the head of Homeland Security walking up to the microphone to hold a press conference after a horrific terrorist attack, but when reporters start asking him about stopping terrorism and catching the culprits, he begins talking about texting and driving." It's an over the top analogy that isn't helpful in the discussion about black-on-

146

black crime.

I do agree with Mr. Harriot when he writes "It is true that the vast majority of black murders are committed by black men, and we should do something to combat that statistic, but that fact has nothing to do with state violence." I completely agree, and stated so earlier as well, but that doesn't mean myself or others should be shouted down on the issue of black-on-black violence.

African American Pastors, and community activists often get shouted down when they use the terminology of "black-on-black crime" as if they are betraying their race. Those individuals shouldn't be silenced, and nor should I. Instead, you should have titled your article something to do with what your third point was about in "We actually do talk about it... all the time." Mr. Harriot points out that "there are countless organizations, activists and movements dedicated to curbing violence in black communities" which is awesome. What Mr. Harriot fails to realize is that most white people are aware of this, and often are out there trying to help as well. Mr. Harriot also insinuates that white people wouldn't know any of this and writes "there's no way white people would know about this unless they stopped deflecting with trite questions and instead actually went into minority neighborhoods to selflessly join the effort to address the problems plaguing..." Ok, you can stop laughing now. Wow, as if millions of white people haven't fought alongside black people to further their cause. As if white people weren't instrumental in the abolitionist movement. As if white people didn't march along with Martin Luther King Jr. during the civil rights era. As if white people don't support the Black Lives Matter movement. There are millions of racist white people out there, but there are millions more who love all people. One thing I am begging black people to stop doing is lumping all "white people" in one category as if we are all Trump supporting racists. It's insulting, and I hear it all the time.

D.L. Hughley, who is both funny as hell, and very intelligent was on a recent Bill Maher episode, and multiple times when talking about something negative, says "white people" this and "white people" that. Fuck, at least say "some white people" I don't want to be lumped in with racist white people, who are in the minority any more than you want to be lumped in with something negative about black people. The last thing I will point out is how Mr. Harriot feels just because someone is white "It ain't none of their damn business." You know what, fuck white nationalists, fuck David Duke, and those red necks who are keeping the KKK alive, fuck people who refuse to acknowledge systematic racist policies that make success much more difficult for African Americans, fuck Fox Fake News, Fuck Kellyanne Conway, fuck Tucker Carlson, fuck the corporations, fuck the lobbyists, fuck the Republican Congress, especially Lindsey (Linda) Graham, fuck Donald J. Trump, but you know what, fuck you too Michael Harriot, you're not helping either.

Conclusion

We are all products of our environment and I don't think ODB was correct when said "it's all good in the hooooood." Aristotle said "Give me a child until he is 7 and I will show you the man." I used to work at an elementary school in the inner city in Niagara Falls, NY. There is a great mix of kids there with many of the kids being African American. One of the kindergarten teachers had a baby so I ended up subbing in that classroom for quite a while. It was crazy because even though the kids were just beginning their academic careers, I felt like they were already so far behind they were never going to be able to catch up. Most of the kids couldn't recognize more than a few letters. The students couldn't spell their own names. I got to work with the kids one-on-one much of the time because even in kindergarten the kids had state testing. I would act really dramatic when they got something correct, and I would tell them how smart they were and fall down on the ground because I was so amazed. Their little faces would just light up, and they were so proud of themselves. Job wise, it was one of the most rewarding experiences I've ever had. I used to get entire kindergarten classes running up to me in the hall trying to hug me when I wasn't in their class. They were such great kids. I subbed in that school for a couple of years, and the change that took place in these kids from kindergarten to 3rd grade was fairly drastic. Their environment had already started to have a negative influence on them. Everything from the way they spoke to their behavior. The environment these kids are growing up in is beyond their control yet it forms so much of their life. Segregation, and poverty again are the continued theme.

Many single mothers do a fantastic job raising their sons or daughters, and often get some much needed family help from grandma or grandpa. However, to say it's not an issue at all would be to ignore the issue. 66% of all African American families are single parent families, while the National average is 40%. African males need to do a better job in being fathers, and/or giving financial support. African American leaders need to do a better job as well. There are so many legitimate reasons why African Americans have it more difficult than individuals who are white. Yet here we are. So, what can we do? We can't go back in time, and do all the things that should have been done. I wish we could, obviously we wouldn't have slavery to begin with. If we couldn't make that change, and started after slavery we could have given African Americans land, proper employment, education, and thus the ability to have upward mobility. The ability to advance for African Americans has been fought tooth-and-nail every step of the way. Unfortunately, we can't go back in time one second let alone years. So let's start from here.

How about mentors in school from kindergarten through 12th grade? The mentorship can start in kindergarten or in the 1st grade, and continue throughout their academic careers. Yeah, I know you're already thinking about the cost, but I'm pretty sure it would be less than incarcerating those individuals who will be able to make better choices at early ages due to professional mentorships.

Yes, professional mentorships; now this is a jobs program I can get behind. Instead of the immoral
150

incarceration jobs program, let's have a moral mentorship jobs program. The entire society would benefit, well except for the prison industrial complex, but you we can easily add them to my list of "fuck you." They should have been in there any way. So, correction officers, judges, and the whole prison industrial complex, a big fuck you too. There, I feel so much better now.

In the past, our government has contributed to segregation through various policies. However, people also self-segregate. When I attended the University at Buffalo I would often meet my brother Mark, and my friends Pete Casler, and Tony Kutis to get something to eat while on a break. I would look around, and be blown away how much everyone segregated themselves. There was literally a distinct white area, a black area, and an Asian area. There was obviously some cross mixing, especially with black and white students, but still for the most part if you were from a certain race, and maybe didn't know many people, you would go sit in the section where people look similar to you. It was the same way in prison as well. This also applies to where people move to. In recent years there have been HUD programs to help integrate people, but often individuals tend to move to areas they are familiar with. The issue with living in those traditionally poor, segregated neighborhoods compared to moving to a suburb is moving to a better neighborhood often leads to better outcomes. If you look at employment rates, earning rates, school test scores, children born to non-wed mothers, the outcomes for black families living in integrated neighborhoods improve. Also, for me the more important issue is what the young kids are seeing

151

and not seeing, growing up in one area compared to another.

I work in sales and marketing for low income seniors. I think about 60% of the people I've met have been white, 30% black, and 10% Hispanic. All the individuals I've met with live in some sort of low income, subsidized housing, and they have all been segregated. If I meet with a white person, they live among mostly white people. If I meet with a black person, they live mostly among black people. Hispanics also live among other Hispanics, but at least from my experience Hispanics are more integrated as far as where they live. Other than where Hispanics live they usually stick around each other because many of the Hispanics who are seniors speak little to no English. Of the better outcomes for African Americans; I'm certain we can add African Americans growing up in the suburbs will also be less likely to be arrested. It's almost 2020, segregation, whether self-imposed or government encouraged, has to end.

When concerning racial prejudice, I'm truly hopeful for the future. With each passing generation racism, becomes less and less prevalent. Think back to my grandfather's generation where racist attitudes were the norm. I doubt my mother would have been able to bring a little black girlfriend over her house like I was able to bring a black, and a Puerto Rican friend over. I'm close with an ex-girlfriend's son who is black, and he has lots of friends who are of all different races. The melting pot theory first surfaced in the late 1700's, but never really fully took place with African Americans. I think this is the century the melting pot is truly taking place. In 1970, only 1% of the population was multi-racial. Today, over 10% of the population is multi-racial. Furthermore, according to Pew the multi-racial population in the United States is growing at a rate three times faster than any other population group in the entire country. As interracial marriage and children continue to rise, prejudice will continue to fall. It's inevitable, but the governmental segregation policy of locking African Americans up is the one issue that will derail all the positives we are all trying to accomplish. Locking African Americans up makes it easy for racist attitudes to feel like they are justified in their racism. Locking African Americans up at young ages makes it nearly impossible to ever become a productive member of society, and holds back African Americans more than anything else.

As I stated earlier, there needs to be a civil rights era type of movement concerning this policy. Locking up African Americans is something our government does on purpose, and many who are participating are not even aware because it's been the norm for so long people who are willing or unwilling participants don't even understand. Individuals such as Senator Cory Booker give me hope that something will at least attempt to be done to get our prison population numbers decreased. It is also important the media keeps the story in the news cycle so it won't just be buried like the souls of countless locked up individuals. CNN's Van Jones does a great job. Keep up your amazing work Van!

Chapter 6-

The Cancer Conspiracy

It seems nowadays everyone knows many, many, people who have cancer, or have died from cancer. Was it always this way? I never heard any of my friend's grandparents dying of cancer. As a matter of fact, in 1900, cancer and heart disease combined accounted for less than 18% of all deaths in the United States. These days, heart disease and cancer account for just under 50% of all deaths in America. My grandfather on my father's side lived to 95, and it was a fall that did him in (or I think he would have lived to see triple digits).

I wasn't so lucky as to see my father live to 95. My father passed away from cancer at 66. Certainly not a tragedy in that he died young, but it was still too young as far as I was concerned. My father was the toughest guy I ever heard of let alone knew. I remember as a kid my father having a tooth that needed to come out but there was no way this man was going to take a day off of work to go to the dentist. I watched my father take a pair of pliers and pull out his tooth, and thought, "he's fucking crazy." My father's toughness came from within in that if something needed to be done there was really nothing that stopped him. Even as an older man he was still a beast. One day at work a 150 pound machine came crashing down on him, breaking his foot. My father again refused to take even an hour off of work so he laced his boot up tight, and went back to work. I'm not saying that was smart, but because his toughness was at some super power level to me, I never in a million years thought something could kill him like cancer did.

My aunt Margie has cancer. My friend Pete Casler's wife Deb has cancer. A number of my friends lost loved ones because of cancer, including my really good friends Mark Dardes and Jimmy Andrews. RIP Mr. Andrews, and Michelle. A few of my uncles have had cancer, but none of their parents had cancer. Cancer seems to be omnipresent these days. So what changed? Is cancer just another needed industry in America that makes too much money to bother finding a cure? Who makes money off of it? Is it also similar to the prison and military complexes in that it's another immoral jobs program?

In Western New York we have many cancer treatment centers with the biggest being Roswell Park. Roswell Park is the first cancer treatment center in America. It was founded by Dr. Roswell Park in 1898, and currently the cancer treatment center employs over 3,300 people. Buffalo is a smaller, big city, but there is a Roswell Park type of cancer treatment center in every city across America. There are also thousands of additional smaller oncology centers employing hundreds of thousands of more people. Even though the cancer industry does employ hundreds of thousands of people, the jobs are just a byproduct of the disease. From everything I've read it doesn't appear to be anyone's motivating factor as it is in the prison industrial complex.

Pharmaceutical companies, our government, doctors, scientists and thousands and thousands of others seem to be looking for cures and ways to prolong those who have cancer. That doesn't mean the Pharmaceutical companies themselves aren't mostly motivated by money. I think the proof is in the pudding there. According to the American Cancer Society childhood cancers make up less than 1% of all diagnosed cancers each year. Therefore, it's just not profitable for pharmaceutical companies to invest much money into cures for childhood cancer. The strange thing to me is even the federal government only allocates 4% of their cancer research funding for childhood cancer. Hmmm, wonder if it's because our government is doing exactly what the corporations tell them to do. Can't make money off the dying kids so fuck the dying kids. No, they don't actually say that, but they may as well.

One of the differences between our grandparent's generation, and the generations that followed them, is that our grandparent's generation didn't consume the amount of processed food that we do; at least not for their entire lives. So is it the food or chemical producing industries that somehow benefits from giving us cancer? Winner, winner, chicken dinner! No, don't eat a chicken dinner, chicken is not so good for you my friend. The World Health Organization declared processed meat as a carcinogen, and puts meats such as corned beef, lunch meat, jerky, salami, bacon, sausage, and hot dogs in group 1 of cancer causers. Group 1 means it's a 100% certainty processed meat causes cancer. In group 2 we have our red meats such as pork, lamb, and beef, and those classified in group 2 by the World Health Organization, and they probably cause cancer (but most experts agree they definitely do). The most common cancers caused by eating meats are breast, prostate, and colon cancers. When you cook meat, the carcinogenic compounds, heterocyclic amines, and polycyclic aromatic hydrocarbons are formed. Saturated fat, cholesterol, antibiotics, and loads of hormones are in the meat you eat. Doctors are often concerned that people are being prescribed antibiotics too often, and thus the antibiotics are becoming less effective. Well, even with millions of humans being over prescribed antibiotics, the vast majority between 65% and 70% are given to animals, and then ultimately, you're consuming them in your meat. Another carcinogen added to your meat to preserve, and add color are sodium nitrite, and sodium nitrate. Consuming too much of these carcinogens can possibly lead to colorectal cancer, ovarian cancer, stomach cancer, non-Hodgkin lymphoma, leukemia, bladder cancer, pancreatic cancer, esophageal cancer, thyroid cancer, and finally heart disease! Fuck that, I'm not eating meat anymore! Oh wait I'm already a vegetarian. If you eat meat, and can't give it up completely, you should at least cut down, and you will cut down your chances of getting cancer and other diseases as well. You can thank me later.

I named this chapter The Cancer Conspiracy because it sounds fucking awesome, right? However, the fact that these huge corporations want to make us sick is unfortunately not even close to a whacky conspiracy theory. Side note, The Cancer Conspiracy was also a progressive rock band from Burlington, Vermont in the early 2000's. They probably love Bernie. Okay, back to the shitty, immoral, greedy corporations who are poisoning and killing us to make billions of dollars. There is a whole history here which tie these companies together. They are subsidiaries, or

157

former companies who changed their names. They are associated with "old money" powerful families, and corporations, but I found myself going crazy doing all the research, and writing page after page of notes. I decided to limit some of the history, and make everything easy and clear. I also found a lot of information tying the Rockefeller Empire into many of these corporations, but it was hard to pinpoint or verify much of the information so I decided to leave them out of it for the most part as well. You can google how they were associated with I.G. Farben in Germany which is the company whom many of the corporations I'm writing about evolved from, and are tied together through. There is so much information, but often times it's this trust or that trust, and then names are thrown in there. It usually makes sense, and it may be true, but there was never any real proof in the reports I read, and it often left me with more questions than answers. I decided to keep it short and simple, giving only information that draws clear lines, and clearly shows how a certain corporation does A, causing B, then sells C to make even more money. No conspiracy here; just real proof.

During World War II, I.G. Farben was the largest chemical manufacturing corporation in the world. I.G. Farben enabled Germany to fight the war, and among other things produced chemicals that helped in the murder of millions. Due to these atrocities a few years after WWII, I.G. Farben was split up. Initially the three corporations it was split up into were Bayer, Hoechst, and BASF with I.G. Farben itself put into liquidation. I.G. Farben's liquidation is a whole other story, but not important to this I guess. Here is a list of many of the corporations that are interconnected into this mess of chemicals, cancer, money, pharmaceuticals, various other chronicdiseases, and more and more money. The corporations include: J.P. Morgan Chase, Sanofi, Clariant, Bayer, Agfa, BASF, Nestle, Bristol-Meyers Squibb, Roche, Procter and Gamble, DowDuPont, Merck and Co. Inc.

If you're looking for one or two devils, or the worst of the worst here, it's definitely Bayer AG and Nestle. We can start with Bayer AG.   I was going to list all of Bayer's subsidiaries until I learned they had 11 pages worth! Bayer manufactures many fungicides, herbicides, insecticides, and pharmaceutical medications. Bayer is all around the globe from their headquarters in their home country of Germany to Dubai, United Arab Emirates, Milan, Italy, Lago, Nigeria, and Misgav, Isreal. Bayer added to its impressive evil empire when it purchased Monsanto on June 7th 2018. Bayer's annual revenue is over 35 billion dollars. How does Bayer achieve these numbers, and what makes Bayer so evil? Bayer starts the process in the ground and the process is completed when you're in the ground. We can also repeat the same process for other players like DowDuPont. Bayer/Monsanto first sells their genetically modified seeds to farmers. The genetically engineered seeds are highly resistant to the Roundup herbicide Bayer also sells. There are a number of problems with GE seeds. The original promise by Monsanto of genetically modified seeds requiring less pesticides, and producing higher yields was a nice promise by Monsanto, but unfortunately for the farmers who purchased Monsanto/Bayer's seeds those promises have not come to fruition. Genetically engineered seeds also require much more water to grow, and in areas where fresh water is not so easily available farmers, use much more of this precious resource than they should. So the farmer buys the GE seeds from Bayer, then Bayer also sells them the pesticides, herbicides, and fungicides. The most well-known herbicide is glyphosate, known and seen in stores everywhere by its commercial name, Roundup. Glyphosate has been linked to over 40 diseases including the big C, cancer. Glyphosate is a broad spectrum, non-selective systemic herbicide. It is often sprayed on fields prior to planting or on crops genetically modified to resist the chemical glyphosate. Glyphosate is known to disrupt the endocrine system, and the balance of bacteria in the gut. Glyphosate can damage DNA, and can be a cause of cancerous mutations. Glyphosate is not only linked to cancer; glyphosate is also linked to hypertension, stroke, diabetes, Alzheimer's diseases, Parkinson's disease, multiple sclerosis, and end stage renal disease.

As previously stated, GE seeds were sold with the promise to increase food production and reduce costs, and since the opposite has happened, we know the real reason for GE seeds is because it's a package deal with Monsanto/Bayer toxic herbicide Roundup. Bugs have also become more resistant to pesticides so farmers use more and more chemicals to combat this increasing problem. In a 10 year span of using GE seeds compared to Non-GMO seeds, framers increased use of herbicides by almost 500 million pounds. Bayer sells such a massive list of pesticides, herbicides and fungicides there's no point in documenting them all here, and to be honest all the chemicals have similar health consequences. For example, the product Confidor contains the active ingredient Imidacloprid, which in high doses in rats led to death, locomotor issues, cardiovascular effects, liver damage, thyroid damage, reproductive toxicity, developmental retardation, neurobehavioral deficits and as always cancer. It should be noted that various studies including the EPA show Imidacloprid does not cause cancer, while others show Imidacloprid indeed does. It also it should be noted that Imidacloprid is considered non-carcinogenic by the EPA, but fuck the EPA, I don't trust those paid off bastards anyway. Most processed foods include GMO ingredients and 90% of corn, soy, cotton, canola, and sugar beet acreage in the United States are all GMO.

There are many health risks concerning the consumption of GMO foods. Some studies performed on the animals that consume GMO's found such issues as: increased allergies, infertility, organ function issues, gastrointestinal issues, and issues with the body's ability to regulate its insulin production. There are also studies out there that potentially link GMO's with autism. I think common sense should tell us that the changes in our food must have a direct link to the staggering rise in autism rates. Growing up, autism was rare. In 2008 1 in 54 boys were diagnosed with autism and that number continues to increase with the number dropping to 1 in 37 boys in 2018. I'm sure you're wondering, so the 2018 number for girls in 1 in every 151 girls; much better but I'm sure we all think it's still too many. Farmers who feed GMO corn to their pigs report seeing behaviors very similar to the traits of autistic children. Studies performed on rats showed rats who ate

GMO food compared to Non-GMO food were passive at times, irritated at other times, and always anti-social. So companies feed GMO crops to their animals, then we eat those meats ourselves thus consuming those mutated genes, and passing them on. Once Bayer has sold all these GE seeds for GMO products, sprayed those crops with pesticides, herbicides, and fungicides, fed those GMO crops to livestock, and then the farmers sell those GMO crops to various food companies who put them into thousands of processed foods which contribute to cancer, diabetes, etc. etc. etc.... then Bayer sells us their pharmaceuticals to enrich themselves even more.

Bayer sells tons of pharmaceuticals to treat everything from pulmonary hypertension to diabetes. Bayer sells cancer treatment medications like Xofigo and radiation treatments like Medrad. Those medications make Bayer AG huge money. So Bayer AG from start to finish collects money on every aspect. Bayer sells the poisons to us, and then sells us the medications to treat it. That is a beautiful business plan. Well, I guess if you own stock in Bayer AG it is, but not so much for the rest of us. People are trying to fight back though. Bayer AG/Monsanto is facing some 8,000 lawsuits!

In mid-September, 2018, Bayer AG had to ask a California judge to throw out a 289 million dollar jury verdict due to glyphosate (Roundup) giving cancer to a school groundskeeper, Mr. Dewayne Johnson. The case was fast tracked because Mr. Johnson has Non-Hodgkin's lymphoma and is in extremely poor health. Bayer AG came out with a typical bullshit statement. Bayer stated "The jury's decision is wholly at odds with over 40 years of real-world use, an extensive body of scientific data and analysis… which support the conclusion that glyphosate-based herbicides are safe for use and do not cause cancer in humans." Sure Bayer AG, we believe you. The question is will money win out as usual or will the judge reaffirm the jury's decision. Who knows what kind of deals and discussions will take place behind closed doors. If the judge reaffirms the jury's decision, what kind of effect will that have on all those other lawsuits Bayer AG is facing? It won't be good and I'm worried that message along with some money will be sent somewhere so that something unjust will happen with Mr. Johnson's verdict.

Nestle, the world's largest food company, is another corporation that has figured out how to profit from poisoning us. Nestle is a really interesting company to look at, and it is so clear they figured out how to capitalize from putting poisonous ingredients into their food. Similar to Bayer subsidiaries, Nestle has too many products to list, and of course there is nothing wrong with that in itself. Starting out, what we want to look at with Nestle is some of the ingredients in almost all of their food products that we consume. We can start with the some of the ingredients in the popular Hot Pockets.

Hot Pockets are inexpensive, convenient, and don't tell anyone, but years ago I use to really love Hot Pockets. Here is a list of the many, many, many ingredients: **Carrageenan**, is an ingredient often used to thicken and stabilize other ingredients in food. The ill effects of carrageenan are somewhat debatable, but there does seem to be some real concerns regarding the thickening agent. Carrageenan may slow blood clotting, and increase

163

bleeding. Carrageenan can cause inflammation and problems with gastrointestinal health. Some researchers have claimed carrageenan is linked to everything from colorectal cancer, liver cancer, to ulcerative colitis. Although some of the information is debatable, and I found an equal amount of studies on both sides of the argument, when it comes to my health I would prefer to error on the side of caution. Fun fact, according to WebMD some people apply carrageenan directly to the skin for discomfort around the anus. Two things regarding that statement. First, visualize that while eating any food containing carrageenan, and you're likely to eat less of it. Second, it states "some people apply carrageenan directly to the skin for discomfort around the anus." The key word being "for," that implies that's why they are applying it…..wtf people. I'm sure that's not the case, but I thought it was funny, anyway………..

Sodium Citrate, used as a food additive for flavor or as a preservative. Sodium citrate issues from this food additive can include muscle twitching, cramps, bloody stools, irritability, vomiting, and weight gain. To be fair the last two side effects can also be attributed to the drunken state you're probably in when reaching for a hot pocket in the first place. **Sodium Nitrate,** another preservative known to increase your risk of heart disease. **Sodium Aluminum Phosphate,** often used as a stabilizer in various processed foods. Aluminum phosphates can be a contributing factor in Alzheimer's disease and other neurodegenerative disorders. **Sodium Phosphate,** is another emulsifier. It's strange to me how many of these thickening agents that companies put in our food are also used as medications to relieve constipation.

We've all heard those medication commercials where at the end the announcer runs through the list of horrible side effects that sound so much worse than the actual problem it's trying to treat, you know, like anal bleeding. Anyway, when you're reading this hear that voice at the end of those commercials. (Make sure you read it quick) Possible side effects include: kidney problems, severe stomach/abdominal pain, mood changes, confusion, weakness, swelling of extremities, chest pain, diarrhea, gas, anal bleeding (oh shit), itching of the tongue, face or throat, and finally trouble breathing. See, wasn't that fun? A little? No? Whatever, neither are those symptoms.

Disodium Phosphate, used to regulate the acidity of food, stabilize and maintain the proper moisture level, and wow, another freaking thickening agent. Disodium phosphate also has some non-food uses including as a flame retardant. As usual some of the issues associated with disodium phosphate are upset stomach and diarrhea. At least now it's pretty clear why Hot Pockets make you go to the bathroom. Other concerns from eating process foods containing disodium phosphate include: kidney disease, heart and lung disease, thyroid issues, liver disease, and finally Addison's disease.

Cysteine Hydrochloride, used as a dough conditioner, increases the doughs elasticity, and helps it rise during baking. I really didn't read anything bad about this as far as your health because it is an amino acid. However, it more than likely comes from human hair bought from barbershops in China. (It's true). Okay, I will end on that light note. There are somewhere near 80 ingredients in a

Hot Pocket, and not all are bad but many are.

Many of these ingredients that Nestle adds to our food has links to cancer, type II diabetes, hypertension, obesity, Alzheimer's disease, Parkinson's disease, multiple sclerosis, end stage renal disease, gastrointestinal diseases, and a myriad of other diseases. Okay, now to the point: Nestle is a food company. Nestle is probably like General Mills, or Kellogg and they use many of these ingredients because they are inexpensive. Well, maybe General Mills, Kellogg, Mars, Coca-Cola, Pepsi Co. all have stock interest in pharmaceutical holdings. Maybe, but unfortunately I couldn't find it. As I stated earlier, this isn't some conspiracy. Bayer and Nestle have direct, clear interest in making us sick, and then treating us, thus making money every step of the way. Perhaps in Nestle's case they saw what was happening, and how the food they produce makes us sick, and instead of changing their poisonous ingredients they jumped aboard the money train. Nestle has subsidiaries, and interests in companies that profit from sick consumers. Nestle Health Science is a wholly owned subsidiary of Nestle which delves into the cure side of the Nestle corporation. Novartis Medical Nutrition is a subsidiary of Nestle who is the second largest supplier in the medical food sector. Vitaflo specializes in nutrition for people with genetic metabolic diseases. Prometheus Laboratories makes devices to diagnose gastrointestinal diseases and cancer. Pamlab offers medical food products for use in nutritional management of patients with mild cognitive impairment, depression, and diabetic peripheral neuropathy. Accera, Inc. discovers and develops innovative
166

clinical applications to address acute and chronic neurodegenerative diseases. Accera, Inc. provides nutrition for individuals with diseases such as Alzheimer's disease. Chi-Med a Chinese pharmaceutical company that produces products for gastrointestinal health. (Nestle has a 50-50 partnership with Chi-Med) Lastly, Nestle invested 65 million dollars in Seres Therapeutics which develops microbiome therapeutics. Just to give you an idea of what kind of money these companies generate we can look at some of their net sales numbers. In 2017, Novartis reported 49.1 billion dollars in net sales. Prometheus Laboratories generates a little above 400 million in annual revenue. You get the point, Nestle isn't in the pharmaceutical business to lose money, any more than it is in the food business to lose money. The reality is, Nestle shouldn't be in either business to lose money. The problem arises when they are linked to each other, and it's in the pharmaceutical company's best interests for the food portion of the business to help make us sick. That's just sick Nestle.

I wanted to stay focused on the companies I found that are using poisonous ingredients and causing us to become sick, but I feel remiss if I didn't at least mention the dangers of sugar. Sugar is in 80% of the grocery products we buy. Companies figured out how much sugar to put into their products so we crave them, and sugar also makes the product itself taste pretty awesome.

However, sugar is horrible for you. For years fat has been made out to be the bigger enemy, but if you're consuming healthy fats it's not true. Sugar is in everything so when your reading those labels be on a sugar count look out. Sugar is linked to an increased risk in diseases such as heart disease, type 2 diabetes, cancer and obesity. Sugar has both physical and psychological effects on us. Anyway, you get it. Do yourself a favor and limit the amount of sugar you intake as much as you possibly can. I promise you, you will be so much healthier for having done so.

Conclusion

As usual, money is in the driver's seat here so anyone that is supposed to be looking out for us isn't. The FDA allows carcinogens like sodium nitrite and sodium nitrate to be added to processed meats, and other foods to preserve them. Carmel color in soda is a known carcinogen, but go ahead and add that too. Microwave popcorn are in bags lined with chemicals, and the seeds themselves have harmful chemicals on them as well. Hydrogenated oils cause cancer, and hydrogenated oils are in tons of products. I used to go through container after container of Nestle's Coffee-mate. I loved Coffee-mate and when I was younger I just assumed a nice wholesome sounding company with a corporate image like Nestle would never put garbage like that in their products. One of my favorite sayings is 'youth is wasted on the young,' and isn't that the truth, especially when it comes to what we put in our bodies. (Including drugs) Coffee-mate has Corn syrup solids, hydrogenated vegetable oil, sodium caseinate, dipotassium phosphate, mono diglycerides, sodium aluminosilcate and God knows what else. I still haven't been able to find a great tasting, decently health coffee creamer. Damn it, Nestle!

It's not just Bayer AG and Nestle who are evil; it's all these corporations who find ways to profit from our misery. JP Morgan Chase has huge stakes in health care industries. General Mills owns more than 100 food brands. General Mills CEO from 2007 to 2017 was Kendall Powell, and Mr. Powell also serves on a number of boards including Medtronic and Catalyst. Medtronic is a heart disease and diabetes medical company which makes the number 1 selling insulin pump. Wouldn't it be in Mr. Powell's best interest to make sure most of those General Mills food brands contributed to individuals obesity, increasing heart disease, and diabetes? Catalyst is even worse. Actually, I'm joking, well, unless you're of the mindset of a Donald Trump. That's because Catalyst is actually a pretty awesome organization which works to help put women into leadership roles at various companies across the globe. So maybe Mr. Powell isn't exactly a bad person, but never underestimate the power of money, and an individual's greed. Mr. Powell is obviously an intelligent, informed individual who surely understands what harmful ingredients are going into General Mills products, and what diseases those ingredients cause. General Mills' Fiber One Bars is the comparative example I always use when speaking to someone about what these companies are doing to their consumers. Fiber One Bars are products that if you are purchasing them, you are assuming you are buying a very health product, but Fiber One Bars contain approximately 30 ingredients, including too much sugar. In comparing all the ingredients in a Fiber One Bar to a Lara Bar, there is no comparison. Lara Bars usually have 2 to 4 ingredients, and you can actually read the ingredients, and know what they

169

are by name. (No need to Google).

As I stated earlier, the FDA isn't looking out for us as they both have a revolving door, and are bought and paid for. Let's look at some other trusted organizations that are supposed to want what's best for us. The American Diabetes Association, nope. The American Cancer Society, nope. The American Heart Association, nope. How about the trusted Susan G. Komen Foundation? Nope, nope, nope, and nope. Clearly, I'm not saying these organizations just do horrible things, but they do follow the money. All four organizations are funded in part by the food industry, and the pharmaceutical industry. All four organizations also promote diets filled with beef and dairy, both of which are contributors to the very diseases these organizations are fighting. Our government isn't looking out for our best interest either. As discussed previously, our legislators get large campaign contributions from Big Pharma, and the food industry so they aren't going to stop these companies from putting known carcinogens in our food.

For fucks sake, our local governments are still putting fluoride into are water supply. Fluoride shouldn't be ingested. Fluoride should be applied topically by a dentist. The fluoride that is added to our water isn't the same as the fluoride found in some water, nor is it a pharmaceutical grade fluoride which your dentist would use. Instead, the fluoride is an unprocessed industrial byproduct of the phosphate fertilizer industry. This type of fluoride often contains elevated levels of arsenic. Have you ever looked at the back of your toothpaste box? Look at it, go ahead, I'll wait…………….. Forget it, I'll just tell you. "Warning: Keep out of the reach of children under 6yrs of age. If more than used for brushing is accidentally swallowed, get medical help or contact Poison Control Center right away." Ingesting a tablespoon of fluoride could potentially kill a child. Make no mistake about it, fluoride is a poison. Why is our government putting it into our water supply? Simple, the fluoride industry, like every other industry has lobbyists, and those lobbyists contribute money to those in power who keep the bs narrative alive. We've all heard the saying "tell a lie long enough, and it becomes the truth," and that is exactly what is happening here. Confront someone with the truth about fluoride, and they most likely won't believe you. The reason being that it's hard to truly change your mind set about something you've always believed in, and have always been told. It's the same reason someone like myself has trouble going from agnostic to full blown atheist.

It's up to us to stop this poisoning. I'm a vegetarian for personal, moral reasons, and people will often say "yeah, but one person isn't going to make a difference." Yes, that's true, if I were the only fucking person! It's simple supply and demand. The more vegetarians there are the more demand there will be for vegetarian products, and the less demand there will be for meat. It's the exact same way with organic products. I try to buy everything I can that's organic. Not that many years ago, the organic section in a super market was small to non-existent. Now when I go to the supermarket the organic section is pretty significant. Organic products aren't that much more expensive. Buy organic, cut down on your meat consumption. If you eat
171

meat four days a week, reduce the number to two or three days a week. In the last ten years, meat consumption has risen by almost 20%. One-fifth of all the greenhouse gas emissions which are man-made come from the meat industry. If you can believe it, that means all those cows, and pigs, etc. are passing so much gas that they produce more greenhouse emissions than the transportation sector. I actually have a friend I believe is contributing quite a bit to these greenhouse emissions as well, but I'm pretty sure his diet is the main reason for that.

Each pound of meat produced also takes huge amounts of water. Each pound of meat produced takes about 10 times the amount of water as some vegetables. If everyone in the United States were vegan for one day a week, it would be as if we magically reduced our collective driving miles by nearly 100 billion miles. The point is; yes, you, as an individual can make a difference because we don't live in a bubble. It's you, and you, and you, and together we are more powerful than even a lobbyist!

Do yourself a favor and be a label reader. Call the 800 numbers on the backs of the product boxes and tell them you want them to stop using a poisonous ingredient when you see it. Stop buying their products! Does it help overnight? No, it takes time. I love Triscuits, but I stopped buying them because they use canola oil, however organic Triscuits do not. I make my voice heard by buying organic Triscuits, and if that's something you care about then you should make your voice heard too. It takes time but in the end the numbers won't lie to these companies. You buy "this", and don't buy "that" then eventually those corporations will produce much, much more of "this" and much less of "that."

You Say You Want a Revolution......well

A billionaire, a middle class worker, and an immigrant are sitting at a table with 1000 cookies. The billionaire takes 999 cookies and turns to the middle class worker and says, "you better watch it, that immigrant is going to take your cookie."

I'm not sure who came up with that, but I love it, and you can change immigrant to a single mother getting food stamps or anyone else getting any type of help. That saying sums up exactly what billionaires/Republicans, try to frame the way of thinking to an easily manipulated, large portion of middle class Americans. The greed of guys like Amazon's Jeff Bezos has got to stop. This guy should be strung up by his balls, swinging from a tree. Most of us live paycheck to paycheck, and I know for myself I can't get out of the crushing burden of my student loans. Okay, we may not want the kind of revolution where we string up guys like Bezos, or do we?? Fine, how about we get Congress to pass Bernie Sanders and Ro Khanna's bill to tax corporations like Amazon, and Walmart for every dollar their low-wage workers receive in government assistance. It will be interesting to see if the rest of the Democrats get behind this obviously fair, and needed bill or will they let the corporations control them as usual.

We need for Bernie to be the Donald Trump of the Democratic Party, and bend the party to his will. It is happening, and we are getting stronger, and stronger with more, and more left leaning candidates winning Democratic primaries, and elections. We have to keep the party moving to the left or we need to have these candidates running as Independents. If the Democratic Party doesn't come aboard who cares? I actually would prefer they did not. We need a legitimate third party to be the norm. Having a real third party is the only way we can possibly get corruption out of politics. So, news outlets I challenge you to start giving coverage to third party candidates. Come on Chris Cuomo, Wolf Blitzer, Alisyn Camerota, and John Berman. Come on Brian Williams, Ali Velshi, and Andrea Mitchell. Come on my hero Bill Maher. Come on Tucker Carlson, and Sean Hannity, okay, there's only a 5% chance the people I listed will ever cover third party candidates, and that drops to zero for Fox Fake News.

One thing I do want to make crystal clear; I don't dislike our troops. I respect them, and what they believe in. It's those in power who lie to them that I dislike. I believe in truly supporting our troops, not just giving lip service to it. Politicians love doing that but then they often desert them upon their return from war. Our troops were deserted after the Vietnam War. Our troops were deserted after Operation Desert Storm where our government denied the existence of Gulf War Syndrome.

Of the almost 700,000 troops who served in the Gulf War, approximately 250,000 troops suffered from Gulf War Syndrome. I believe the best way our government can support our troops is to not put them in harm's way for no reason. That's what I want for our troops. If a U.S. soldier is going to risk their life, then it needs to be something worth risking it for, not oil or our corporation's profits. It needs to be a just war, i.e. WWII. I don't criticize this country because I hate it, I criticize the United States government because I love our country. I just want it to be as beautiful as its ideals are. I want those in power to represent the people, not the corporations. I don't really want to string Jeff Bezos up by his balls. First off, sorry Jeff, but I'm not touching your balls. Mr. Bezos just announced he's going to raise his starting pay to $15.00 an hour, which is a great start. Mr. Bezos is still way too greedy though. I started writing this book being motivated by anger. I want to see change. I can't take all these injustices any more. Maybe it won't help at all. Maybe I can will a small difference in writing this book. We can all make small changes and together make a difference.

Writing this book has been emotionally painful at times. During the Trump administration, our country is more polarized than ever. I've lost many friends who I've known for years. They weren't the person I thought they were and I have been vocal in my calling out of Trump and any racist or immoral behavior. I guess I've insulted many, and in return their ignorance and racism broke my heart. There were times while researching I had to stop, and take a deep breath. The people who suffer at the hands of our might are real people. I saw many disturbing photos. Sometimes the photos were of Noam Chomsky's "unpeople" who were missing limbs from bombs dropped years ago. Sometime the heartbreaking photos were of children crying over their dead mother or father's body. We go about our lives, and what do we worry about? Getting a better job or maybe a nicer car? Our problems are real, but unless a family member is sick with cancer or something along those lines, our problems tend to revolve around material things we don't have. What most Americans pray for is so different compared to what someone who was born in a third world country worries about.

If there has been an "unpeople" here in the United States, I suppose that would be African Americans. There is no shortage of heartbreaking photos or films revolving around the treatment of African Americans. From lynchings to beatings just because the color of their skin. I love the movies Mississippi Burning, A Time to Kill, Birth of a Nation, 12 Years A Slave, and The Help. Watching those movies is emotionally draining, but they aren't fiction, and they aren't ancient history either. One of my top five favorite books ever is Frederick Douglass's My Bondage and My Freedom. My Bondage and My Freedom should be mandatory reading for every high school student. I think it could go a long way to eliminating any racist thoughts. It is such a powerful book, and can be life altering. Education and knowledge are always the key. Knowledge of what's happening throughout the world. Knowledge about what's happening in our own country. If you see the hypocrisy, if you see the truth, how can you not want to make a change?

Public Service Announcements

Don't Impede My Right to Speed, if you are in the fast lane, speed or as Ludacris said "move bitch, get out the way, get out the way bitch, get out the way." Seriously, if the speed limit is 65 and you're in the fast lane doing 60 or 65 you should be shot. Yes, really, shot! (Okay, shot at?? Just to really scare them, then a good talking to?)

Say "thank you" when a stranger holds open the door for you, rudeness infuriates me! Do you think it's someone's job to open the door for you? No, it isn't so if a stranger holds the door for you, say thank you, or you are obviously a complete, rude, asshole. (Probably a Trumpster).

Use Face Lotion, if you don't use lotion on your face you probably look ten years older than you are, or than you should. Do yourself, and everyone else a favor, and use lotion.

Put Your Article All On One Page, If I google an article, and then I go to read it, and have to keep hitting "Next," and "Next," and "Next," then guess what? I'm not reading your freaking article.

Get a Real Job State Troopers, stop stealing the money of hard working people just trying to get to work on time. You steal our money so you can have a pay check. You're the biggest welfare collector of all.

When Going Up An Onramp to Get on the Throughway........Look!!!!!!, Don't wait til you're at the last 50 feet of the onramp and then start panicking, looking how you're going to get in the lane. Look as you're going up the onramp, you not-knowing-how-to-drive mother fuckers!

Stop Texting While Driving!, I have to drive a lot for my job and I can't believe how many people I see with their heads down, staring at their phone, texting away and never, ever looking up. You're going to kill someone! I always hope they have a close call that will wake them up and make them see the text can seriously wait.

Student Loans!, 20 years after I graduated, and I still owe over $60,000 dollars in student loans. The last 5 years I've been paying over $300.00 a month with not one penny going toward the principle. Student loans are financial slavery for over 44 million Americans who owe approximately 1.5 trillion dollars! Instead of bailing out the banks our government should bail out those with student loans. It would allow those millions of Americans to spend more money in their communities, improving the lives of themselves and many others in the process. (Sorry, that one wasn't really a PSA, but I hate the feeling of drowning in my never ending student loan debt and I had to vent).

About the Author

    James considers himself a Bill Maher type of Liberal. In other words, he's going to speak the truth, and if you're offended you might need to toughen up or go get a hug from your mom. Often times liberals' unwillingness to speak the truth for fear of looking as if they are not the super liberal they think they are just stops things from getting done. James earned a Bachelor's degree in History from the University at Buffalo, and a Master's degree in Secondary Education from Niagara University. James was a professional boxer, and although talented for various reasons James ended up a journeyman fighter. James, along with Ken Cosentino, Liz Cosentino, Bill Kennedy, Marcus Ganci-Rotella, Baird Hageman, Sunny Sharma, and Gary Marino own the film production company "White Lion Studios." James starred in "Crimson: The Motion Picture", and had a supporting role in the hilarious "Attack of the Killer Shrews!" James also owns the t-shirt company Tortured Tees. Tortured Tees are designed for motorcycle and tattoo enthusiasts. Tortured Tees, for the tortured soul in all of us. James hopes this book is both entertaining and educational, and inspires you to make any small change which will create a small, but significant difference in someone's life.

180

Made in the USA
Columbia, SC
19 February 2019